Practical
PARENTING

*A Common Sense Guide
to Raising Cooperative
Self Reliant and
Loving Children*

STANLEY SHAPIRO
KAREN SKINULIS
RICHARD SKINULIS

EDITED BY
JODY ISENBERG

Practical PARENTING

Copyright © 1996 by Stanley Shapiro

Published by Practical Parenting Program Inc.
Toronto, Canada
E-mail: parent@interlog.com

Cover Design and Text Layout:
InZane Visual Communications Inc.

Canadian Cataloguing in Publication Data

Shapiro, Stanley,

Skinulis, Karen,

Skinulis, Richard

      Practical Parenting

ISBN 0-9681352-2-6

FIRST PRINTING 1996, 3,000 COPIES SOLD
SECOND PRINTING 1997

PRACTICAL PARENTING STUDY GUIDE
ISBN 096813520X • FIRST PRINTING 1996, 2,700 COPIES SOLD

ADVANCED PRACTICAL PARENTING STUDY GUIDE
ISBN 096813528 • FIRST PRINTING 1996, 1,200 COPIES SOLD

Dedication

*We dedicate this book to the
memory of Rudolf Dreikurs,
who not only inspired us,
but helped us understand
the important principles
that this book is based on.*

Acknowledgements

*Our heartfelt thanks to
Sheila Shapiro, Corey
Finkelstein, Kelly Frances
and Betty Denaburg for
their continued assistance,
support and encouragement
throughout these last
four years*

This book came to be because of my firm belief in the education of parents. Through my 35 years as a father, teacher, family counsellor and school psychologist (in the United States), I have come to realize that the relationship parents have with their children is more important than any other. Virtually every developmental problem — from bed wetting to Attention Deficit Disorder — can be helped if parents were only taught the skills they need to be effective.

Another firm belief is that these vital skills should not be available to a few, but to everyone in the community — whether they have educational training or not. With that in mind, *Practical Parenting* has been designed to be read on its own, or used in conjunction with the *Practical Parenting Study Guide*. Although this book can greatly benefit any parent or care giver when read separately, I feel it's greatest impact will be felt if it is used in classes of parents eager to be the best that they can be — who want to bring the benefits of enlightened parenting and democratic principles into their family's daily life.

Stanley Shapiro

CONTENTS

Practical PARENTING

Y ou belong to the first generation of parents who see parenting as a job. The proof is all around: parenting books, magazines and experts abound, as do parenting classes. Like any job, parenting is a skill that must be learned through training. Of course, every parent since time began has loved her children. The immediate bond and urge to nurture is powerful and instinctive when you first cradle your newborn. This is something you don't have to learn. But the fact is, *love is not always enough.*

Humans, whatever their age, are mysterious and complex beings. When you stop and think about the awesome task of teaching and raising a human being, it is astounding that we have taken it so lightly, with literally no preparation or thought as to how it could best be done. The reason, of course, is that we usually raise our children the same way we were raised — autocratically. It usually went something like this: The parents laid down rules and the children either followed them or they were punished. In some ways, this method worked relatively well, mainly because all adults agreed this was the best way. They were guided by clichés such as: "Children should be seen and not heard", and "Spare the rod and spoil the child". The father was the head of the household, just like a head of state, followed by mom as second in command. It wasn't until the spread of the ideas of democracy and equality, along with the questioning of things like racism and sexism in the middle of the 20th century, that the family itself experienced fundamental change. The result is that the ideals of social equality have percolated down to finally include children.

The definition of social equality is: Every person has the right to make a choice, and is responsible for the consequences of her decisions. Every person has the right to be treated with dignity and respect regardless of her social status or age.

Dignity and respect means that each person is entitled to be treated in the same manner that she wants others to treat her (sometimes known as The Golden Rule). Another way of expressing the concept is — you should treat every person the way you would treat your very best friend.

All social groups are struggling for these equal rights. The impact of this on today's families has been deeper and more fundamental than most of us realize.

Children have come to understand (through the media and also by watching their parents interact) that they are entitled to equality and respect, even though they are not the same as adults in terms of experience or knowledge. That's why even very young children will confront their parents by saying things like: "You can't do that to me!" Older children have even been known to get a lawyer in order to reinforce their rights. This new type of family dynamic calls for a new approach to child rearing. We have to learn the skills that are needed to raise children properly — especially in a society that is engulfed in rapid change — while working toward equality within a democratic system.

Freedom, choices and order

In order to create an atmosphere conducive to social equality, the relationships between family members have to be based on democratic methods. Democracy means people have certain rights and freedoms, but these freedoms are connected with order, following the rules, and accepting responsibilities for their choices. Therefore, freedom implies responsibility. Allowing people to do whatever they want is known as anarchy.

Democracy means that people are equal partners in relationships and in solving the problems of the group. They have the right to be heard, have input into decision making, and have decisions based on consensus.

These changes to the way families interact are challenging. But as often happens, these challenges to the family are also a great opportunity to raise our children better. It is our firm belief that learning effective parenting skills will go a tremendous way towards producing more loving, socially responsible people, as well as more harmonious families.

S U M M A R Y

- Parenting is the most important job you will ever have. Like all jobs, it is made up of skills that must be learned. Until recently however, no one thought it necessary to learn how to be a parent. Doing it the way they were raised was considered sufficient. Unfortunately, love is not enough.

- In the past, most families were autocratic — the parents laid down the rules and the children obeyed or were punished.

- The spirit of democracy and social equality has spread far enough to finally include children, and a new and better way of raising families has emerged.

- Democracy means people have rights and freedoms, but also that they are responsible for their choices.

- Social equality means that every person is equal, and has the right to be treated with respect and be included in decision making (of the state, the family etc.).

What do parents want for their children?

I magine your children as adults. Now imagine what attributes you would ideally like them to have. The list would probably look something like this:

I hope my children are self confident, with high self esteem. I hope they are considerate of others, and not always thinking of themselves. I hope they cannot only find their passion in life, but live up to their potential. I hope they have a keen social interest, and give to the community what needs to be given. I hope they have both the desire to be cooperative with others, and the skills to do it. I hope they are responsible enough so that I can rely on them. I hope they are strong and self sufficient. I hope they can grow up to be good parents themselves. But most of all I hope they are happy, and I know that these traits are what they need to achieve it.

This list varies from family to family, but according to famed psychiatrists and theorists Alfred Adler and Rudolf Dreikurs, the key to happiness is in mastering The Five Tasks of Life:

1. Friendship
2. Work
3. Love (intimacy)
4. Self Acceptance
5. Spirituality (searching for the answers to the great mysteries of life)

To master these five life tasks, your child will need a solid grounding in self esteem and social interest, as well as the social skills required in their particular culture.

Developing social interest

> "Ask not what your country can do for you. Ask what you can do for your country."
>
> — *John F. Kennedy*

Parents today often make the mistake of thinking that their job is to make their children happy — by buying them things, letting them have their own way, giving them constant attention, taking them places, and fulfilling their every need. The trouble is, this approach fosters a feeling that "only my happiness is important". The child is not learning how to make *others* happy which, ironically, in the end is the only thing that actually makes *him* happy. That's because when you focus on yourself, true happiness can never be attained. People who are self involved suffer more — they dwell on problems and their little pains and discomforts. But caring about others takes you out of yourself and actually decreases unhappiness. Another word for this is social interest.

Social interest — one of the basic tenets of every major world religion — is the ability to concern yourself with the interests of others as well as yourself; to care what happens to them and how they feel. One of our prejudices against children is that they are self centred and don't care about others, but this is not the case. We have observed many instances where children spontaneously demonstrate social interest.

> *It's 5:30 p.m. and three-year-old Liam is hungry. He marches into the kitchen to demand some food. He sees that dad is busy making dinner. Instead of bothering him, he asks if he could help wash the lettuce.*

Liam already instinctively recognizes the needs of the situation. He can see that dad is busy and he knows dinner will be ready soon. His job is to pitch in and help. His mom and dad have helped him achieve this by encouraging him to be independent, by being consistent about meal time, and by not always giving in to his immediate demands.

This is important because people with social interest have empathy with their fellow humans — they can see through others' eyes and feel through others' hearts. When you teach your children to care about others, as well as recognizing the needs of any given situation, you are also giving them the tools to enrich their own lives.

> *Ten year old Shawna has energetic parents and two older siblings. Every Sunday Grandma comes over for a big dinner and then the family cleans up. "Give me a hand clearing the table Shawna," Grandma says. "Aww, but my favourite TV program is on. Can I do it later?,"*

she asks. Mom jumps in: "That's OK. It's her favourite show. We can clean up here."

Later, Shawna comes in for some water and sees the family efficiently working together in the kitchen, talking and laughing as a group. Although she wouldn't know how to say it in words, Shawna feels separate from them, and unsure of how to make a helpful contribution. They are all bigger and better than she, and don't really need her help, she's sure.

Just then, Grandma holds out a dish towel. "I need some help here Shawna. You dry and I'll stack."

Shawna demures. "But my show is on."

"That's too bad," Grandma says, turning back to the dishes. "It would be fun to talk while we clean up."

Shawna likes talking with Grandma and reluctantly begins to help. Soon, however, she's absorbed in her work. After the job, Shawna has a feeling of satisfaction and accomplishment.

Frequently, Shawna had been excused from chores because she is the youngest member of a "take charge" kind of family. Although she enjoys being pampered, she has not yet learned to enjoy helping people. It will take some time for Shawna to change. The family can help by expecting her to pull her own weight, and by convincing her that she can do it. Although social interest is innate, it still has to be encouraged.

Do not do for children what they are capable of doing for themselves.

When children are not expected to contribute to the family, there can be serious repercussions:

1. They expect service from others.
2. They do not have a chance to develop the practical skills needed for independence.
3. They develop a belief that it is their right to be excused from responsibility.
4. They may not want to do anything that is not fun, which can interfere with their working hard at school or doing homework.
5. They can become angry when asked to do something.
6. They do not appreciate the hard work that goes into making a comfortable home.
7. They don't develop the sense of worth that comes from being useful.
8. They will always look for the easy way in life.

One good way to encourage social interest is by example. This means that parents should always treat each other with respect and demonstrate consideration for neighbours, peers and extended family.

Sometimes, in our materialistic society where the most important thing is to buy the right kind of running shoe, it's hard to get children to give. So let your kids see you volunteering for neighbourhood groups, giving of your time and money to charity, participating in school events, being hospitable to guests, or coaching a children's sports team.

Years ago (before mid century), children were expected to contribute more. Larger families meant that the older ones had to look after the younger ones. And, with more families living on farms back then, the chores that children did were crucial to the success of what amounted to a family-run business. Today's small families, urban existence and the emergence of technology have all worked to relegate children to the role of passively playing and going to school, not as integral and useful members of the family. The challenge parents face today is to give their children the feeling that their contribution is essential.

This fostering of social interest in your children is very closely related to self esteem. If children feel that their contributions don't count, that they don't really belong, they may begin to feel inadequate and suffer low self esteem.

Your self esteem is how you evaluate yourself — your feelings of self worth. We monitor this constantly and in many areas: morally, "Am I a good person?", intellectually, "Am I smart?", emotionally, "Am I happy?", socially, "Am I liked?", the ability to achieve, "Am I a good parent?" etc.

In order for us to love others we must first love ourselves. In the same way, children have to feel good about themselves in order to behave and cooperate with others. The best way to foster feelings of high self esteem within children is by being encouraging.

Good self esteem means that children feel they are valuable in and of themselves — that they are worthy human beings just as they are, not in some hypothetical future after they have worked on themselves, but right now. When their self esteem is high, it is much easier for them to improve their behaviour and learn new social skills.

Note: Don't mistake self esteem for self concept — an objective inventory of yourself: "I'm 5'10" tall, I'm a woman, I have red hair, etc.", always made in comparison to others.

Your self esteem is the chief governor of what actions you will take throughout your life. People with high self esteem do more, take more risks and as a result, are generally more successful. People with high self esteem also have more choices in life. For example, if you think you can learn, you may choose to go to university, teach yourself, or not go at all. With low self esteem, the first two choices don't even seem possible.

We all want our children to have high self esteem. The most important factor in achieving this is encouragement *(See Encouragement, Chapter 4),* and the biggest culprit in lowering self esteem is criticism.

> *Three year old Sheila wants to help clear the table. Her parents reluctantly agree.*
>
> *"OK, but be careful. Don't drop anything. You know how clumsy you are."*
>
> *Sure enough, Sheila drops a glass and breaks it. Mom hits the roof.*
>
> *"I told you to be careful. Now look what you've done."*
>
> *Sheila's face twists in anguish as she contemplates what she has done. She bends over to help clean it up, but Mom pushes her away.*
>
> *"You'll only cut yourself. Let me do it. You just go watch TV or something."*

Sheila has a natural desire to help and the courage to try new things. She has watched other people clear the table and believes she can do it too. She has made a leap of faith that should be encouraged. What is a broken glass compared to the chance to maintain a three year old's self confidence. Besides, that's what plastic dishes and cups are made for. Mom should have welcomed Sheila's offer to help. Instead, she only reluctantly agreed, pointed out that she is clumsy and then would not let her help fix the mistake. Think how this entire episode could have been used to build Sheila up instead of pushing her down.

Sheila asks to help clear the table. Mom agrees.

"That's a great idea Sheila. I'm so busy I could really use the help."

Beaming, Sheila carts things back and forth. She drops a glass which shatters on the floor. Her face drops, but Mom is unfazed.

"That's OK honey. Get your shoes on and we can clean it up together. I'll use the broom and you hold the dustpan."

After the glass is cleaned up, they continue to clear the table as if nothing had happened. Sheila has not only been allowed to be a productive member of the family, but realized that mistakes are not the end of the world. She has even learned how to sweep up.

Some children have areas where they have naturally high self esteem and others areas where they do not. They may try to overcompensate, restricting themselves to areas in which they feel secure, and avoiding activities they don't.

Eleven year old Pedro wants to build a doghouse for his pet cocker spaniel, Coco. He tells his father about his plans. "That's a great idea, I'll bet you can make a terrific dog house." Dad is careful not to take over the project, only providing direction where Pedro's inexperience would hold him back.

Obviously, Pedro has high self esteem in the areas of technical skills and ability to learn. However, he has low self esteem in social situations.

Pedro has reached the age where he is invited to mixed parties. But he is so socially uncomfortable that he finds large gatherings of people painful. He stutters, blushes and spends a lot of time staring at his shoes. He is even awkward when relatives come to the house for a visit. What makes him much more relaxed is being alone and working on one of his projects.

Pedro is an only child born to older parents and hasn't socialized much. His parents have to create more opportunities for him to be around people so he can build up his social skills: inviting over friends that he gets along with, joining team sports and school clubs. Good communication about his feelings is also an important step. Instead of brushing these problems under the rug, give him a chance to talk about it, to share his problems *(See Communication, Chapter 7)*. He also needs to see what is right with himself, not what is wrong. If he has a good sense of humour or is a loyal friend, point out to him that other people value these things.

- All parents want their children to be happy and successful. The way to achieve this is not to give them everything they want, but to build up their self esteem and instill in them a sense of social interest.

- Social interest is about concerning yourself with the interests of others. You teach social interest by example, by letting your children do for themselves and others, and by letting them know their contributions are important.

- Self esteem is our evaluation of ourselves — our feelings of self worth. People with high self esteem have more self confidence so they do more, take more risks and have more choices. We bolster self esteem in our children by being encouraging. We lower self esteem by criticizing, pampering, and showing a lack of faith.

- A few generations ago, larger families meant that children had more responsibilities and received less attention. Today's smaller families, along with the emergence of technology, have resulted in children being relegated to merely going to school and passively playing. The challenge to parents is to let their children know that their contributions are vitally important to the family.

- Don't do for children what they are capable of doing for themselves.

Influences on the personality

Although science has made great strides in the areas of psychology and genetics, the degree to which heredity and environment influence our personality has not been decided. Children are born with genetic information encoded in them, information that could cause them to lean towards one end of the personality spectrum or the other. Some children for example, are born active; they enjoy movement, seek more stimulation and interaction than children who are born with more of a passive nature, who are quieter and able to sit for longer periods of time. Mothers we know report that some babies kick and squirm *in utero*, while others lie quietly, content with only a fraction of the activity.

Some people argue that either genetics, or sociological factors (or a combination of both) determine personality. But if that were true, all of the mystery of life would disappear. How is it that someone born into severely underprivileged circumstances can rise above it to achieve spectacular success and happiness? How is it that someone born with a physical handicap can become a concert musician or a professional athlete?

The environmental influences fall into two broad categories: social and familial. The social category embraces the social situation the child is born into: developed or underdeveloped country, race, religion, urban or rural, war or peace. Except for the later example, none is necessarily better than the other.

Self determination

We believe the missing ingredient in this genetic-environment formula is the interpretation that the *child* brings to her particular life situation — her sheer creativity and drive. In other words, we all, no matter what our age, make choices and to a great degree determine our own futures. And that's where the influence of the family — parenting styles, the amount of encouragement, the level of social interest and the intensity of love — comes into play. The family works with the clay of the child's creative forces — whether he values hard work or gives up easily, cares about others or is self centred, solves problems well or turns to frustrated anger. Everything a child is born with and into has an impact on personality. But for the purposes of this book, and notwithstanding self determination, the familial is by far the most important.

The family

The influences of the family consist of the parents or primary care givers, and any extended family that the child encounters daily. They are the first social unit the child is exposed to. He learns about all aspects of life through interactions with his family: mother, father and siblings (and grandparents, aunts and uncles if they actually live with the family). The outside world reaches the young child through the filter of the family.

Family life can be broken down into five areas:
- The family constellation.
- Family values.
- The family atmosphere.
- Parenting style.
- Modelling.

The family constellation

The Family constellation is defined as the relationship of each sibling to the other.

The Five Positions in The Family are:
1. The only child.
2. The oldest.
3. The second born.
4. Second born becoming the middle child when the youngest is born.
5. The youngest child.

It's important to understand that although a child's position in the family constellation is not a personality determinant, it is a significant influence.

As you can see, with each new birth, a new family configuration forms and each relationship takes on new meaning. Therefore, each position in the family has certain unique characteristics. Each position has its advantages and disadvantages and it is impossible to say if it is better to be in one position or another. The children's birth order affects their perceptions, interpretations and evaluations of the world. It gives each child a specific place in the family, and specific expectations and responsibilities. This is one of the important reasons why no two children grow up the same in any given family. Have you ever wondered why the same family can produce one child that is the picture of cooperation, and another that is always looking for trouble? They have the same family environment and the same parents. Besides their genetics, the only other major differences are their own interpretations of events and the order in which they were born.

Charlie is the first born to parents who are what could be called overachievers. They are both successful executives who have not only survived but thrived in the exacting corporate world. They have high standards for themselves and also for their children, for whom they have high hopes and want only the very best. Performance that puts them in the middle of the pack will not be good enough. They provide lots of early, structured training (like music classes and second language instruction), and watch them closely, always ready to correct a mistake in grammar or lapse in table manners. There is a lot of criticism and yelling when things aren't done right. They feel they are being hard but fair — an approach they feel will be the best for their children in the long run.

Charlie has a sensitive nature and his mother's petit stature. He is slower than average in his language and motor skills, which worries his parents. His innate clumsiness results in lots of falls, accidents and broken dishes. *His parents redouble their efforts to make Charlie more competent and independent, but they are already worried that he won't be quite good enough to make the grade. At an unconscious level, Charlie knows his parents aren't all that happy with his performance. At two years old, he is still eager to do things but can't always accomplish what he wants. He has trouble climbing the ladder to the playground slide and gets frustrated easily. This is compounded by his parents barking commands like: "Come on Charlie! You can do better than that! You're not trying hard enough!"*

When Charlie is one and a half, Jonathan is born. He sees the baby being coddled and paid attention to. Like a lot of kids, he starts to regress, acting more like a baby and having tantrums. His parents — under stress from lack of sleep and increased parental work load — get more and more disappointed with Charlie and sharper in their reprimands. Jonathan is a physically bigger child than Charlie and more quick to learn. Mom and Dad show obvious pleasure with his rapid development, and quietly think to themselves: "This is more like it."

Jonathan quickly learns that by developing his skills, he gets Mom and Dad's approval. He also understands (at an unconscious level) that Charlie's progress is not as quick as his own, even though Charlie had a head start. This makes him feel very confident in himself. His language and physical skills are catching up to those of his older brother. This self confidence carries over into the social realm, where he begins to develop an outgoing, gregarious nature, making friends easily and feeling comfortable around people.

Charlie watches his brother's progress with a sinking feeling. Jonathan's successes are starting to make him feel inadequate. In what is known as "social competition", children constantly compare themselves to their siblings. They eye each other very closely and watch to see if they are gaining or falling behind in each area of development. If discouraged, they will avoid participating in the areas where the others are strongest. Charlie, for example, abandons even trying to compete with his brother in physical activity. On the positive side, Charlie discovers that he is good at drawing and making clay models. Instead of trying to compete with Jonathan in sports (where he doesn't excel), he concentrates on his artistic abilities. His dad, who also likes to draw, takes a particular interest in this. Charlie has finally found something he is good at. He has become a quiet, more introspective person. His (unconscious) thinking is: "If I can't be the life of the party like Jonathan, I'll be the good guy, someone you can count on." So Charlie tries hard to please and be pleasant. He has fewer friends than Jonathan, and they aren't the most popular children, but he forges strong bonds with them and develops a level of intimacy that Jonathan does not know.

Two years after Jonathan was born, Mom gives birth to a baby girl. Lara is what Mom had always secretly wanted; a delicate, pretty girl she could dress up and relive her own childhood with.

Because she immediately becomes "the little girl" of the family and therefore special, she grows up being pampered and showered with attention. As a result, by age two, she has become a demanding and wilful child. Despite her tantrums and misbehaviour, she is still

Mom and Dad's little darling, getting away with things (particularly from Mom), that from the two boys would never have been tolerated.

The family's expectations for Lara are not very high. Ironically, because there is so much less pressure on her, she ends up doing well in school. Although the boys go along with the role of her being the cute baby of the family, there is a certain amount of resentment of the attention and preferential treatment she gets. Charlie sees Lara as another threat, an attack on his already weak self image from another point of the compass. As the only girl, she is innately special. Plus, like Jonathan, she has a strong personality and he doesn't feel able to compete with her on that level either. But as her interests begin to develop, Charlie finds to his delight that they share a love of the arts, in particular music and books. Slowly, they begin to bond (an alliance between alternate siblings — first and third, second and fourth etc., is common but not necessarily the rule). As for Jonathan, Lara has taken away his status as the youngest and most adorable. He became even more set in his brash, outgoing ways. Since Lara is not in the least interested in sports, Jonathan continues to hold down the role of "most likely to succeed".

Six years later, Jessica is born. Typically, the social competition begins to wane when there is a five to seven year gap between siblings. Although Lara feels somewhat ambivalent at Jessica's birth, she doesn't feel all that threatened since her own role is so firmly established. Jonathan and Charlie take a more paternal attitude toward this new baby. It is almost as if Jessica has been born into a family of five adults and is being raised from a psychological point of view because she is not in competition with her siblings, as an only child. There is a great deal of excitement generated by this unexpected newborn. The family crowds around her. There is someone to hand her a bottle or pick her up at the slightest squawk. Jessica enjoys this service and attention and grows comfortable with her role as "the baby". She quickly learns that in order to keep getting this kind of attention, she need only maintain her helplessness. For instance, she doesn't learn to walk or talk until relatively late, mainly because she doesn't have to. If she wants a toy, she need only make a noise and point at it. As the years pass by, she develops a dependent and babyish personality. She waits for someone to zip up her coat or read her a book. She is by far the most passive person in the home. There is a large age gap between Jessica and the other siblings, so their basic personality (usually set by the age of seven) is largely unaffected by her.

By his teen years, Charlie has become a bit of a loner. He enjoys activities he can progress at on his own terms, not those of a group. He likes chess and drawing and is beginning to aspire to being a commercial artist some day. He and Lara spend a lot to time together and encourage each other's ambitions.

Jonathan is rarely at home as a teenager. He is totally engrossed with team sports and an ever widening circle of friends. Despite showing a lot of promise, he has some trouble buckling down to work, unlike Charlie who has good concentration skills and does well academically.

Lara feels secure in her role as the "eldest girl" and has a particularly close bond to Mom. Her significance in the family is so obvious and secure (almost a second mom), that she doesn't feel she has to compete with her two brothers, and in fact, is free to learn from them. However, her close friendship with Charlie has become an alliance against their common threat: the middle child Jonathan's social and athletic success.

Jessica is not really part of the "pack". Her parents don't have the energy to spend as they did on the first three children, and have not been as consistent or as firm with her. The result is that she is the most pampered, and as a teenager, she has no more future ambition than to work at the local fast food restaurant with her friends.

We hasten to add that *this is only one example* of how the family constellation of two parents and four children could work. Every family is different. For example, if Charlie's parents hadn't been so demanding, he might not have given up so quickly on his physical development. He probably would never have excelled at this, but his overall personality would have been more confident. Jonathan, following in the footsteps of a more encouraged first born, might have become a trouble maker in order to gain significance. His gregarious nature might have turned him into the class clown, in contrast to his "good" older brother.

Lara, seeing that the role of the difficult child was already taken, might have become the "helpful" child, the only girl to help mom in a family of males. Her alliance with Charlie would still happen, to keep Jonathan as the rebellious middle child.

Jessica, instead of enjoying the babying, could have just as easily rejected her role and worked twice as hard as everyone else to catch up and even gain superiority.

Personality types in the family constellation

All children are unique, but here are some common characteristics for each child in the family constellation:

The Only Child

"Birth order is never considered to be a determinant. The child has the creative capacity to choose his role in the sibling relationship; his place in the family constellation, but we must always determine how the child has perceived and used his place."

— Dreikurs & Soltz, 1964

An only child is just that; a child that lives in an adult world. Because of this, the only child will probably strive to gain approval from adults more than children that have brothers and sisters. There are two major ways for the only child to be recognized: approval can be gained either by being proficient (like adults), or by soliciting sympathy through helplessness or shyness. We stress that the following are only propensities, and that in the end, it is the child's interpretation of his role in the family that is important.

The only child may:

- try to be the special centre of interest outside the home because she is used to this being her position inside the home;
- not have to compete with siblings for the favourite position as the "favourite" child, and therefore, might be less competitive in nature;

- have a feeling of belonging without having to prove herself;
- develop good verbal and other skills because she lives in an adult world;
- become "socially curious" about life in homes with siblings and may therefore, enjoy socializing; or
- be used to and be comfortable with spending time alone and therefore, be good at entertaining herself;
- be self-centred because she lacks the give and take and sharing that happens in larger families;
- have many wants fulfilled without effort;
- be overprotected;
- have parents who are more anxious about child raising (the confidence of parents increases with number of children);
- be more indulged materially;
- get her way more often then others;
- lack social skills in play.

The First Born Child

The only child is the centre of the parent's universe. Think of a triangle, with two arms of the triangle reaching down to a point which is the child. The birth of the second child alters this cosy relationship for all time. Going from only child to first child is often a big shock. Now, the favoured spot has been usurped. He is dethroned!

Unless she is extremely competent, the first child could become discouraged because there are greater expectations from the first born. Parents of first borns are less experienced and more likely to be anxious. The first child may enjoy behaviour such as:

- a burning desire to be "first", to gain and hold superiority over younger children;

- if she has feelings of inadequacy, she may feel unloved and neglected when she is dethroned by the new born. She may then switch to being the "difficult child";
- being more serious;
- staying on tasks.

She may have the tendency to align herself with the adults and therefore be:

- more conservative;
- more authoritative;
- a natural teacher;
- bossy;
- the icebreaker who paves the way for the younger children. She might do things like walk to school by herself first, but also date, work and leave home later because the parents are more anxious and reluctant to let go.

The first child may:

- be given more responsibility;
- develop more leadership qualities;
- develop good organization skills;
- be comfortable with authority figures;
- have adults take them into her confidence;
- feel she belongs to the adult world more than to the child's world;
- be a high achiever.

The Second Child

The second child may try to catch up with her older sibling. It is a race in which she feels under constant pressure. The second child always has before her another child who shows more advancement. The second child may feel uncertain of herself and her abilities if the first child is successful.

The second child is almost always the opposite of the first child. If the first child is the "good child", the second child may become the undependable, "bad" one. If he is following a conscientious child, he may be happy go lucky and irresponsible.

The second child may:

- be charming with good social skills, and be fun loving and playful. Often she is more liberal later in life, and can be more rebellious;
- be more independent at a younger age;
- be more socially competent because she was born into a social situation;
- resent being bossed around by her sibling and may grow up to dislike authority;
- be more irresponsible because there are others over her who will take on the responsibility.

The Middle Child

Some middle children feel uncertainty about their place in the family. They may feel that all the rights and privileges go to the oldest child, and that the youngest gets away with a lot. The results could be:

- feeling unloved, or "squeezed out";
- finding their place in the group more difficult.
  However, they could develop good mediation skills by being in the middle;

- the middle child is not as noticed, and can more easily do her own thing. The extremes (first and last) get more attention, leaving the middle child with less stress, pampering and expectations. By being forgotten, the middle child has less pressure to succeed.

  She can become discouraged if she has both a capable younger and older sibling. On the other hand, if the oldest and youngest are having difficulties, the middle child can become the capable one.

The Youngest Child

This child holds a special place in the family constellation. Always seen as "the baby", she is cute and helpless at first and may even grow to enjoy this. If that happens, the youngest may:

- adopt a babyish way of speaking;
- find ways to illicit service from others by being helpless;
- be late in her developmental stages (talking, walking etc.);
- have the least responsibility;
- talk a lot about "growing up" and becoming "big".

The youngest can become very discouraged because everyone is so far ahead of her. She can give up the idea of ever catching up, and therefore, become a more dependent personality.

On the other hand, being so outdistanced may prompt her to strive for success — to catch up to everyone; (think of the biblical story of Joseph and the Coat of Many Colours). If that is the case, she will become very ambitious, to the point of becoming president of company etc. She wants to be the "leader" and not the "baby".

Other influences on sibling development

What we have been talking about so far has been the chronological order of sibling birth. But there are other important influences that help shape the personality of siblings. One of them is age gaps. The closer in age the siblings are in the family constellation, the more intense the competition. If the children are as little as 14 months apart, the youngest can catch up quickly and therefore, pose more of a threat to the older one. On the other hand, siblings who are further apart in age don't benefit from the camaraderie and common interests those closer in age have. As we have already mentioned, children that are more than seven years apart have almost no sense of social competition.

Gender can also bestow upon a sibling a very special significance in a family. Siblings of different genders usually have less competition. A large family of boys who finally produces a girl (or vice versa) automatically give her a unique role. Or, in a family where all the siblings are the same sex but in which there was a great desire for one of the opposite sex, one sibling may be given the part. So one of six girls may be a "tomboy", or one boy of seven may act more feminine. (Keep in mind that this is a role she is playing, and does not necessarily have anything to do with sexual orientation.)

Demonstrating family values

The values a family has are created when one or both parents take a strong position on an issue. When such a position is taken, children have to make a decision whether to accept or oppose it.

Kimberly and Michael love sports. In fact, they met on the tennis court. Their idea of fun is to go on a long bike ride, or cross country ski. Table talk during meals often revolves around levels of fitness and equipment. The TV is usually tuned to a baseball game. Kimberly leads a lunch hour aerobics class and Michael plays squash three or four nights a week. Their children, Tom, Gord and Melanie, grew up in the gym and the back seat of a bike. They have caught their parents' enthusiasm for sports, and the family uses this mutual interest as a focus for doing things together.

Obviously, sports and physical activity have become family values in Kimberly and Michael's family.

Some of the important issues upon which parents take a position are: education, religion, honesty, sociability, sports, music, charity, sharing, caring, helping, winning, empathy, money and material possessions. Even if only one parent believes in a particular thing, it is still considered a family value.

In order for a value to have impact, children must observe the parents actually following through with the value, not just talking about it. If a parent says that it is important to learn to read but is never seen reading a book, it is really not a family value.

Of course, if children become rebellious, one of the areas they might fight the parents on is the family value.

Carlo and Maria are self made people who struggled to make a success of themselves. They feel that being neat, clean and well dressed is one of the most important things in life, in that it is a mark of success and self respect. Their friends share this view. They both want their two boys, Anthony (11) and Justin (13), to be spotless and colour coordinated at all times. From an early age, the parents bought their clothes for them and told them what to wear and when to wear it.

The boys are rebellious in general, but they have decided to rebel against this particular family value very strongly because it is where they are pressured the most. They have decided to go along with the fashion dictates of their peers instead of their parents. They wear torn jeans and T-shirts no matter what the occasion . Regular and intense arguments over clothes fill the house, especially when there is a social function involving the parents' friends.

Had Carlo and Maria not been so insistent on what clothes the children wore, the boys might have been more cooperative, at least on special occasions. No parent likes her children to look messy or dirty, but it probably would have been easier to get the boys to comply if some consideration were given as to what their likes and dislikes were. Not doing this caused the family value to become a source of conflict. The antidote is offering a choice. When it's time to get dressed up to go out, Carlo and Maria could offer the children a small selection of clothes they feel would be appropriate and ask them: "which of these clothes do you want to wear?" As the children get older (six years old and up), they could be included in shopping for their clothes. Being able to pick and veto new clothing will let them feel that *they* have chosen the clothes, and alleviate the feeling that they are being dominated. It will also allow them to go along with some of their parent's suggestions. Although they may never adopt this particular family value, it will be a lot easier to get their cooperation.

The three parenting styles

There are three basic parenting styles: **AUTOCRATIC**, **PERMISSIVE** and **DEMOCRATIC**. What differentiates these styles, is the question of where the power lies. In the autocratic style, the power lies with one or both parents. In the permissive style, power lies with the children. But in the democratic style, the power is shared with everyone who is a part of the family.

Autocratic

The underlying philosophy of an autocratic home is that people are not equal (someone has most or all of the power and it is this superior person that makes all the decisions, passing down the law from on high). This is the traditional family set up, and it is only with the spread of democratic principles — mainly during this century — that this old hierarchal approach has begun to whither away.

The leader of an autocratic family may receive his or her status because of his or her position as the bread winner, or may be looked upon as the strongest or the smartest. In some autocratic families, the father might be the overall head but he may relinquish power over some areas, such as the raising of the children, to the mother.

One hallmark of the autocratic family is that there is much less cooperation than in a democratic family, mainly because family members don't have to solve problems themselves, just follow the orders of the leader. The head of the family might occasionally ask for advice, but in the end, he or she makes the final decision. He or she dishes out the rewards and he or she imposes the punishments (and there are a lot of rewards and punishments in autocratic homes). This leads to more competition between the family members in order to gain the favour of the all powerful autocratic head. Of course, no one can punish the boss, so everyone has to be very careful. They walk around on egg shells, trying to please the boss, especially if he or she happens to have a temper. This creates a certain atmosphere of anxiety. There is also a feeling of resentment and powerlessness, because the rules cannot be changed and the children's views are not taken into account.

If the family leader is more of a "benevolent dictator", there could be a lot of affection and closeness in the family atmosphere, but this is usually tempered with the underlying fear of punishment. This can create a distance, and even a love-hate relationship because the hugs make you feel close, but the punishment pushes you away.

Whatever tone the autocratic leader takes — benevolent or not — the children of the family study this person the closest. For many, being the top dog looks like the best position to be in so they strive throughout their lives to be the superior person and to set up autocratic atmospheres in their homes, work and social situations. Unfortunately, this attitude precludes cooperation, which even leaders need to be successful. In the modern world, cooperation is the real key to success, and the democratic ideal is the best way to foster it.

Permissive

The word permissive comes from the root word *permission.* When you are permissive you are giving your children permission to do whatever they want. The main objective of this kind of parent is to make her children happy. If the children cry when it's time to go to bed, she lets them stay up. If they ask for something, she gets it for them. These are child-centred families. The child of permissive parents is given a tremendous amount of freedom, the most negative being the freedom to do as she pleases without considering the group. Any family is, at its core, a group that has activities and jobs it must do together. If the child is allowed to go her own way, she is no longer a functioning member of the group, and will not learn how to cooperate with others, a crucial skill for a successful adult. Permissive parents are usually pampering as well. They do all the chores and bear all the responsibilities. The children are not expected to chip in.

Permissive parents want their children to like them, to be their pals. They have also found that sometimes it's easier (in the short term at least), to let the child decide when to go to bed or have dinner. Another motivation is that some parents who were brought up in very strict families, have vowed not to inflict this kind of parenting style on their offspring. It could also be that the parents themselves don't like being restricted by schedules and routines, preferring the freedom to be spontaneous.

The end results of the permissive parenting style are children who haven't learned how to plan ahead, who are poorly organized and who think of themselves first. They haven't had to learn how to do that much so they lack skills and patience. They tend to deal only with the wants and desires of the moment (what *they* want to do not what needs to be done). But the world is not nearly as permissive as their families are. People raised in an "anything goes" atmosphere can be angry a lot of the time, with their friends and with life in general because they can't always get their own way like they used to.

One possible extreme result of this permissive approach is a child who is a little tyrant. When the time comes and she goes out into the world to join the group, she won't like being told what to do. For example, she doesn't like games because games involve rules and cooperation. She can become stubborn and resentful when told to do her homework. And she easily becomes angry with her friends when thwarted. This is because she has been trained to be considerate only of herself, not of others.

Democratic

In a democratic home, the family members see each other as more or less equal; that is, with rights and opinions and a say in the decisions that affect their life. The main feeling is one of mutual respect that comes from believing that everyone is an equal partner in an enterprise called "the family". This does not mean that the parents don't have the final say in crucial matters such as finance or child safety. But it does mean that family members listen to each other better and more often. That's because, with no one person lording over the roost, they have to make decisions together continually. And, with all decisions affecting their lives being consensual, members of a democratic home tend to cooperate more in problem solving.

How To Be Democratic

A discussion with children younger than five is inappropriate in many instances. For example, they simply haven't mastered the concept of time yet, so it's hard to figure out with them how many hours of sleep they need. Instead, concentrate on things like establishing routines *(See Competence and Independence, Chapter 11)* and being consistent. And keep in mind that, although you have to make some decisions yourself for younger children, you have to be aware when they are finally ready to understand and accept the responsibility of their choices. Then explain to them the facts of the situation in as few words as possible. They can then make the decision themselves. In this, as in most things, timing is important, as well as staying tuned in to your children's development.

Six year old Fiona wants to walk to her friend's house, which is six doors away. The family lives on a busy street with a lot of pedestrian traffic. Until now, her parents have walked her to her friend's house. But they have been giving her a lot of "street proofing" lessons. She has been asking for some time to walk by herself to see her friend. The fact that Fiona is a cooperative child who shows a keen sense of responsibility brings her parents around to the decision that she is ready. Watching surreptitiously from the window, they let her go. When she gets home, she is obviously proud at this milestone in her life.

In a democratic household, if the parents don't want the kids to watch something, maybe it's too violent or too adult in nature, the reasons why are explained to the children. By stating your case, you not only get the children to do what you think is best without coercion, but you use the situation as a learning experience. Of course, this is more work, because instead of merely giving them a command, "No! You can't watch that! It's too violent!", you have to take the time to help them understand why it's not good for them to watch certain things at certain ages. The hope is that the child will internalize the reasons for these restrictions so that eventually, the motivation for not watching certain things comes from *her*, not just a command from you.

The way to approach the family's weekly TV viewing is to have everyone sit down with the TV Guide and decide what she wants to watch. Set up a schedule, and make sure that it includes the parent's schedule. The family will have to come up with rules, such as no TV until everyone's homework is done etc., but make sure you reach these decisions together.

How three different parenting styles handle "The Great TV Debate"

The TV is a central appliance in most homes. Problems about who watches what and when can reach epidemic proportions. How you handle it is a good indicator of what your parenting style is.

Autocratic

In this home, the parents are very worried about their children watching violent or adult programs, as well as too much in general. They have come up with a list of shows and viewing hours that they feel are suitable for children. The children complain that other kids watch the "good" programs, and a lot more of them per day.

Permissive

This system is even simpler. The kids watch whatever they want whenever they want to. The parents defer to the children about what is watched, and there is no monitoring as to what is appropriate or inappropriate. Bedtime is often delayed deep into the night if something good is on. Because there are no rules, the TV stays on constantly, whether anyone is watching it or not.

Democratic

In the democratic system of parenting, the entire family discusses the weekly TV schedule. This means the kids have an input and so do the parents. For younger children (five and under), you have to make the decision for them, but make sure you give them some choices — "Do you want to watch The Big Comfy Couch or Sesame Street?" — so that they feel they are a part of the process.

If there are conflicts (and there always are), teach your children how to work out a compromise: "What would you think about watching your show this week and Jimmy watching his show next week?" The key is to suggest a compromise, not inflict one.

When everyone helps set up the schedule, there are bound to be programs she wants to watch that you don't want her to. If the show contains material you feel would damage young minds, such as extreme violence or sexuality, you can put your foot down and ban it from the schedule. But you also want to teach your children common sense as well as how their choices have consequences. For example, let's say your eight year old wants to watch a scary program. It's not too extreme but you know it will affect her. The fact that she will have the thrill of being scared out of her wits is why she wants to watch it in the first place. Put it to her this way: "If you watch it and you have nightmares or trouble going to sleep, you won't be able to watch it again. Does that sound fair to you?" You are making a deal with her instead of giving a command. And, since you are pretty sure she *will* have trouble going to sleep, you are teaching her to trust your judgement.

Using a show that is not too scary may help her to avoid watching a show (perhaps at someone else's house), that is much more horrific. It's a little like a vaccination where a weak version of a disease is injected into a person to help build defense against the full blown version. What you have going for you is the fact that consequences are truly the best teachers there are. If you just tell her, she doesn't really learn why, but if she tries it and suffers the consequences, she *knows* why. Besides, if you can't get the child to agree with the rule or decision, resistance to it will come up again and again. In the democratic system, having the child learn and accept why a particular decision is made prevents the problem from occurring again and again.

Discouraging family atmospheres

As parents, you create the atmosphere of your family; its tone, feeling and level of harmony. You create this atmosphere by everything you do, beginning with how you treat your spouse. Your children look to you for models of how relationships work. In fact you define for them what a relationship is. They pay attention to how you make decisions together, how you demonstrate respect for each other, and even your tone of voice. A lot of their ideas about how they relate to other people will result from how the family atmosphere affects them.

The Over Protective Atmosphere

Parents must protect their children from the dangers of life, especially when they are too young to know themselves. But the over protective parent has so little faith in her child, that she tends to smother her in a cocoon of safety that prevents her from learning how to take care of herself. The over protective parent has an anxiety attack if her child wants to go down a slide that is over four feet high. She can't bear to have her play on the sidewalk for fear she will dart out into the street, or use a pair of scissors in case she cuts herself. Some parents literally follow their children around, arms outstretched to be able to rescue them at a moments notice.

As we have said, the world is full of dangers, but the overprotective parent exaggerates these dangers. She often can't let her children out of her sight. This shows a lack of confidence, which can make the child overly fearful and insecure. These children can grow up never learning how to cope with different situations.

Five year old Monica goes to the playground with her father. She sees all the other kids running, jumping, swinging on the monkey bars and going down the big slide. With a look of pure joy, she starts going across the monkey bars hand over hand herself, but Dad has visions of catastrophe. "Better come down from there honey," he says. "That's too high for you. Why don't you play in the nice sandbox?"

Monica gets tired of the sandbox and heads towards the slide — not the little kids slide but the bigger slide, which other kids her size are playing on. Dad follows her, keeping up a steady stream of advice and anxiety-laden exhortations. "Climb slowly honey. Hang on tight. Don't go down too fast. I'll catch you at the bottom."

Monica gingerly descends, a look of worry on her face the whole time. Eventually, Dad steers her back to the safety of the sandbox.

Dad is so overly concerned with safety that he can't let Monica enjoy the normal activities all the other children are engaged in. Watching them from the sandbox, Monica feels left out of the fun, and a little bit different than the other kids. Dad is teaching her that life, for her at least, is very dangerous, and it is better to watch from the sidelines than to participate. Of course Dad does have a point; the playground is a place where children do sometimes get hurt. But our job as parents should be to teach our children how to deal with the danger. Obviously, you must prevent serious injury, but a scuffed knee or a small bruise can mend and be learned from. Allow your child to learn from experience.

The overprotected child has trouble taking risks which, when the risks are undertaken sensibly, greatly increases her chance of success in most life tasks. On the other hand, the child's reaction to this kind of domination may be to take too many risks and behave in a reckless way.

The over protected person (just like the overindulged child we will talk about later), is inherently a pampered person. The pampered person wants things to be easy. She has been trained to expect this by her pampering parents. But it is a terrible preparation for life, which can be a frustrating struggle. Pampered people tend to be uncooperative and self centred. They also have more problems getting along with others, tend to be more demanding and angry because their demands often are not met. The attitude of the pampered person is: "I'm special. Therefore, I should get my way."

Parents can pamper their children not only by doing everything for them, but also by not expecting too much from them.

The Overindulgent Atmosphere

Another way parents pamper is by overindulgence. Quite simply, the parents give the child everything she wants: if she voices an interest in having a birthday party at Disney World, the reservations are made. If four barbie dolls are not enough, a fifth is snapped up immediately. A good tip off of this is the child who greets the parent every night when they come from work with a cheery "what did you bring for me?" Overindulgence is not just about material things like toys, but letting children stay up late when they want to or paying a lot of attention to them when they want it.

This kind of pampering parent can't stand the thought of her child suffering even a little bit, often because she didn't have that much when she was young. Another reason is that it is a way of dealing with an unpleasant situation: giving a whining child what he wants is a good way to stop the whining, especially if it's in a public place like a shopping mall. Yet another reason is to ensure the child's affection. This puts the child in the driver's seat and, although giving your child responsibility is important, having a three or an eight or a twelve year old in charge is not a good idea.

That these parents love their child is not in question, but they mistakenly believe that the way children develop into happy people is by getting what they want, when in fact the opposite is true. The most unhappy people are the ones with the most needs. That's because even for successful people, life is usually a matter of getting too much of what you *don't* want and not enough of what you *do* want. Being able to go to school or work when you don't feel like it is something you have to learn how to do. Happy people have developed the ability to deal with this, and they didn't do it by having their every wish fulfilled as a child.

The negative effects of overindulgence can be a "what's in it for me" attitude, where the emphasis is not on social interest (what are the needs of the situation and how can I help?), but on getting what *you* want. This kind of pampered child tends to whine and complain a lot; to argue with her parents and friends, and at life in general, because life isn't continually bringing her the presents and attention she has become accustomed to receiving.

The Competitive Atmosphere

Being competitive is not only a common family atmosphere, but one of the driving forces behind western culture. Crowds at sporting events chant "We're number 1"; parents want to know where their child ranks in her class, or ask their child after the big game, "did you win?" To a great degree, you are judged by your performance. It is the erroneous belief that if you are not a winner (and we mean number one, not number two), you are a loser, and less of a person for it.

This is a hard belief system to overcome. After all, every parent wants her children to succeed and do well. But judging a person's worth by how well she measures up is not healthy. Improving yourself, or wanting to win the game is fine, but there is something wrong with feeling depressed, or bad about yourself just because you lose a game or a contest.

Although competition between siblings is natural, competitive parents can foster it to a dangerous degree by comparing and contrasting performance: "You got three wrong on your test? Tommy always got perfect on *his* spelling." It can happen in countless, subtle ways: "Why don't you keep your room tidy like Janice does?", or "Come on, swim out to the raft. Robin can do it and she's a year younger than you."

The first questions competitive parents ask at the end of the day are things like: "How did you do on your test? Did you win the game? How are you doing in math? This lets everyone know what is important and what is not. The question is never "Did you have fun?" or "Did you learn anything?"

A non-competitive family would be content with a B average. A competitive family would not. Everyone wants her children to do well in school. Helping them see the fun and satisfaction in learning gives them the tools to fulfill their potential. Of course, the children of competitive homes can become highly skilled and hard working people. But they can also suffer tremendous anxiety: always worried if they will do well enough to meet their own or their parents' high standards. They don't have much lightness or fun in their work because after all, their goal is always to be the best. Someone else can always be better than you, so the accomplishments of others is a constant threat.

Life is very serious for the overly competitive. They have very high standards and are often never satisfied, and may feel like a failure even when they do very well. The toll of being overly competitive can be anxiety, being a workaholic, or even alcohol or drug abuse. The truth is, many of these competitive people might have been even more successful, and more fun to be around, if they had been less competitive. The major flaw in this kind of approach is that you are always comparing yourself to others.

The Critical Atmosphere

In the critical atmosphere, the parents constantly remark about the children's behaviour or work, usually what's wrong with it. There is an underlying tone of disappointment in this approach to parenting, an unhappiness with the child (in extreme cases this can even manifest as disgust). This kind of parent has very high standards. The message is: "No matter what you do, it has to be done without flaw".

The main problem with this approach is that the child may internalize the criticism and go from "The work is not good enough", to: *"I'm* not good enough because I'm imperfect".

This kind of child will be afraid to take chances because he fears making a mistake. He will do things in order to please instead of because it needs to get done; playing up to whatever he sees as the higher power "the authority" in his life. He may develop impossibly high standards himself, with all the dissatisfaction and disappointment this entails.

If the parents are extremely critical, the child might feel that no matter what he does, it will never be good enough: "I got five As and one B and that's not good enough. I'll never be able to pull it off." This can develop into the kind of child of whom everyone says: "She is bright enough and has the potential to do well, but she just doesn't try hard enough."

Generally speaking, she has low enthusiasm levels and doesn't really know how to enjoy herself.

If a child from this kind of parenting atmosphere has good self esteem, he can become a very competent person, but the fear of failure will always be there. Think of the "A" student that is always stressed out.

A highly critical, perfectionist parent can find fault in anything. He doesn't like the way his child eats his soup, or the way he combs his hair, or keeps his room. He finds fault with his taste in books, friends and music. He eats too slowly or too fast or drinks too much milk or not enough. It can also be a subtle criticism that exists mainly in the tone of voice, which is often angry, disappointed and exasperated.

Tommy comes to the table for dinner.

"Tommy, what took you so long, I had to call you three times."

"Sorry."

"Don't tell me you're going to come to the table with that dirty T shirt. And wash your hands, they're filthy. How many times do I have to tell you."

He comes back with a clean shirt and hands. He sits down at the table and grabs some bread.

"Tommy. Wait until everyone sits down. Honestly."

"Ralph. Look at what the baby is doing with her food. Do I have to do everything around here?"

Suzy asks for some stew.

"Say, please may I have some stew.'"

Mom now gives a little lecture about eating a balanced meal, eating slowly, etc.

"Tommy, stop playing with your food."

Betty boasts that her team won the baseball game by six runs. "It's not important who wins, but how you play the game," Dad intones.

A child spills his milk. he is given a well worn lecture about being more careful. The children have heard it so many times most of them don't even hear it any more. They are told to sit still, stop fooling around, stop making faces at your brother. The whole meal consists of one infraction after another.

This may sound like an uncommon nightmare but it happens more than you think. In fact, the kind of atmosphere a family has can be most easily seen at meal time, when the whole family is doing something together.

The Rejecting Atmosphere

In the absence of warmth there is always doubt. You may love your children, but if you never show it or tell them, they can't be blamed for thinking that maybe you don't love them. Parents who are cold, distant and unemotional towards their family can instill the belief that they are not wanted, or are uncared for. Remarks such as: "I'm going to find another family for you to live with", can have devastating effects on children if the family atmosphere is cold enough to make it seem possible.

Three year old Samantha has her water colours out on the new rug. Her mother catches her and hits the roof. "Bad, bad girl! How could you do that to our brand new rug! I'm going to leave you on somebody else's door step!"

Samantha is crestfallen and runs to grab her mother's leg while protesting that she is sorry and will never do it again. Mom shakes her off her leg and stomps out of the room. "I don't care if you're sorry. I don't even want to speak to you."

A more subtle problem arises when parents talk glowingly about a cousin, neighbour or sibling. In a warm, supportive family the child should be able to handle it, but if a cold, rejecting atmosphere has created that grain of doubt, the child is left to think: "They love him (cousin, sibling, neighbour, etc.), but I'm not good enough to love." That is because, in the absence of loving support, the child feels inadequate. It's not necessary to say bad things about her, the absence of good things will be enough.

Children need hugs *every day*. They need words of affection, and reassurance and just plain love *every day*. The best way to show your love is simply to make time for them. Some parents may have trouble doing this. They are too business like, or too wrapped up in outside interests to spend time with their children. Not being available is also a form of rejection. Spending time with someone means you like him.

> *Bobby runs up to Dad and tries to give him a big hug. His dad is busy trying to fix the toaster and is feeling preoccupied and frustrated. "Stop this nonsense! Can't you see I'm busy?"*

In the rejecting atmosphere, the child feels that, unless she makes the grade, the parents will not love him. In a warm, affectionate family, the child feels that no matter what he does, parental love will always be there. It is unconditional, even when he has messed up.

This kind of parent might have come from an emotionally cold home himself. His only models were cold people and so he thinks that this is the way parents should act. Or, an overly pampered child might grow up to being easily frustrated by the demands of child rearing. He has grown up used to having his own way, to having things easy. But raising children is not easy and involves sacrifices that pampered people might not be willing to make, hence the resentment and outside interests. Another possible reason for rejection is an unwanted pregnancy.

One possible result of this kind of family atmosphere can be a child who feels that he is not lovable ("even my parents don't love me"). He may feel that he himself is somehow bad. He may have trouble getting along with people, or may see others as bad or untrustworthy. His movement would always be away from people. Depression could also be a problem. In other words, he generalizes that how his parents felt towards him is how everyone else feels about him.

Of all the possible family atmospheres, the rejecting atmosphere is the worst. In extreme cases it results in children who grow up to be criminals. In fact a lot of violent criminals felt they weren't loved as children.

The rejection atmosphere descends into outright abuse when hitting is involved. Just as damaging is emotional abuse. "You're such a wimp! Stop crying or I'll give you something to cry about!"

If someone hit you, you would charge him with assault. If he talked to you this way, at the very least you would leave and not have anything to do with him. Children deserve the same rights to safety and respect. We believe that parents who use these methods to discipline their children need to seek outside help to improve their parenting skills.

Modelling

Children look to the parents in order to see how they should act. For instance, if there is a frustration, how should it be handled? By calmly finding a solution, or by yelling and throwing things down in anger? If the parents smoke, doesn't it make sense that the children will too? Is hitting someone when you are angry or upset all right? How should you get along with your friends or your spouse? By being cooperative and considerate? Or by always trying to be the boss, or striving to "win" at the relationship?

Children also watch the relationship between the parents. They pay attention to who (if anyone) has a dominant position. This will give them ideas about male and female roles. Remember, only one generation ago, women's and men's roles were very clear cut and rigid. These days gender roles are moving towards a state of equality, and your children will be learning this from you, just as you learned gender roles from your parents. Other things they learn from you include: being quiet or talkative; critical or not critical; negative or positive. They watch how you solve problems and what makes you afraid. Even subtle things such as facial expressions and how you walk will be picked up and imitated.

There is also a lot of negative modelling that goes on. If the child does not like the way the parent is, he may make a conscious decision to not be like that parent. For example. A strong willed, rebellious child might observe his weak willed, submissive parent, and resolve to never be like that. This child will take a stand and never back down. He might also have trouble having respect for anyone who isn't strong and aggressive.

- Environment and heredity may have some influence on the development of a child's personality. But it is also important to factor in the choices the child makes, and this is where the influence of the family is the most important — the degree of love, encouragement or discouragement the child receives.

- The influence of the family can be broken down into 5 areas:
  1. The Family Constellation   4. Family Values
  2. The Family Atmosphere   5. Parenting Styles
  3. Modelling

- The Family Constellation is the relationship of each sibling to the others. A child's position in the family constellation has significant influence on his personality. The position of the child changes with each new sibling, and each position has its advantages and disadvantages.

- The five positions of the Family Constellation are:
  1. The Only Child
  2. The Oldest
  3. The Second Born
  4. The Second Born (becoming the Middle Child when the Youngest is born)
  5. The Youngest

- Each sibling strives for ways to succeed and feel significant, and watches the strengths and weaknesses of the others closely.

- Other influences on personality within the Family Constellation are age gaps between the siblings (the closer in age the more intense the competition), as well as the gender mix.

- The positions that the parents take on certain issues (a love or ambivalence for sports, neatness, cooperation, selfishness etc.) become family values. These values affect the child's personality development in one of two ways — he will either embrace them or rebel against them.

- There are three distinct parenting styles:
    1. Autocratic   2. Permissive   3. Democratic

- The autocratic parenting style is parent centred. The family members are not equal and all of the power lies with the parents. There is less cooperation and more competition in this kind of family.

- The permissive parenting style is child centred and gives the children permission to do whatever they want. The main objective of this style is to make the child happy. The drawbacks of this style are:
    1. there is little routine or rules;
    2. children don't learn to cooperate (because they don't have to);
    3. children don't learn to plan ahead.

- The democratic parenting style is family centred. The family members all see each other as social equals, and everyone has a say in the running of the family. Parents still have the last say in areas such as finance and safety. Democratic families are more cooperative and better at problem solving.

Discouraging Family Atmospheres:

- <u>Overprotective</u> parents try to protect their children from all of the dangers and sufferings of life and tend to exaggerate these dangers. They lack faith in their children and prevent them from experiencing and learning.

- <u>Overindulgent</u> parents give their child everything he wants, from toys to attention. This cultivates a "what's in it for me?" attitude.

- <u>Competitive</u> parents teach their children to judge their self worth by how well they measure up, instead of doing things for the fun of it, or to learn, or out of interest, or to help.

- <u>Critical</u> parents constantly remark about a child's behaviour or work. The main danger with this atmosphere is that the child will begin to internalize the criticism and make the leap from "the work is no good,' to "I'm no good".

- <u>Rejecting</u> parents may very well love their kids but can't show it. They can also make the mistake of showing more affection for a particular sibling or relative. Children should know their parents' love is unconditional, not dependent on performance.

Modelling:

- All children look to their parents to learn how to react to different situations. They copy our effective and ineffective behaviours.

- Negative modelling refers to children who do not like certain characteristics of their parents, and who resolve to not be like them.

The four goals of uncooperative behaviour

The Reasons For Uncooperative Behaviour

C hildren are uncooperative because they are discouraged. This simple truth is at the heart of any successful attempt to correct a child's uncooperative behaviour. All inappropriate behaviour is an attempt by a discouraged child to find significance, as well as her place in the group. The job of the parent then, is to understand the motivation that is at the root of inappropriate behaviour, and then help the child find more constructive ways of belonging.

Significance

Significance refers to whether or not the child feels a sense of belonging; whether she views herself as being in a plus or minus position.

This is easy to say but often hard to do. Parents are often baffled as to why a child will repeatedly do something she knows is wrong. The fact is, children often don't have a good understanding of their own behaviour. When asked why they won't eat their dinner, their answer is often a very honest "I don't know." That's because the mistaken goals of misbehaviour are unconscious; i.e.; the child is not aware that she is seeking undue attention, or power, etc.

There are in fact four goals of uncooperative behaviour: Undue Attention, Power, Revenge and Assumed Inadequacy. When your child misbehaves, he is trying to attain one of these goals. Understanding this concept is the key to understanding your child's motivation, and is an invaluable tool to becoming an effective parent.

There are four goals of uncooperative behaviour as coined by Rudolf Dreikurs. Virtually every time your children misbehave, they are trying to attain one of these four goals:

1. Undue attention

2. Power

3. Revenge

4. Assumed inadequacy

Once we understand the unconscious purpose of the child's behaviour, we can begin the process of effectively dealing with it. When we are unaware of the child's motivation we tend to act experimentally to try to find a good way to respond. When our response is not effective and the child repeats the action, we use power methods to control the child. These methods are frequently damaging to the parent-child relationship and to the child's self esteem.

Handling uncooperative behaviour

In dealing with uncooperative behaviour, the parent has to think about both the short and the long term. Your short term goal must be to handle the behaviour at the moment it is happening. The long term strategy involves ways of overcoming the discouragement that caused the uncooperative behaviour in the first place. It's important to have the answers to both at the beginning.

The parent's job is to help the child change uncooperative behaviour to cooperative behaviour. To do this, you first have to make sure that the child does not receive a payoff. In other words, you don't want him to reach his goal. If he does, he has no reason to change. Often it's easier to deal effectively with the immediate behaviour, while ignoring the long term goal of encouragement. Children are very good at finding alternative ways of reaching their goals. For example, you might be able to stop a child from eating with her mouth open to gain undue attention, but she might simply start fighting with a sibling and still attain the goal. So your long term strategy has to be one of helping your child overcome her mistaken goal. You do this by building self esteem, creating social interest, and helping children feel they belong without always being in the limelight, as well as using the appropriate strategies at the moment. In order to figure out what the appropriate strategy is at the moment of uncooperative behaviour, we need to diagnose the goal.

Diagnosing

Diagnosing uncooperative behaviour is as important in child rearing as getting the correct diagnosis from your doctor in order to deal with a medical problem. If every time a patient came to a doctor complaining of a headache and the doctor merely diagnosed a migraine and prescribed a sedative, she would be missing countless other possible causes and their treatments. In understanding a child's uncooperative behaviour, it is more helpful to understand the motivation of the child than to simply punish or lecture. Only if you understand *why* the child is misbehaving, can you help her overcome it. Keep in mind that the same behaviour can have completely different goals. For example, one child may whine for attention, while another does it to gain power. Refusing to eat could be done to attain the goal of inadequacy by one child, and for revenge by another.

Even the four goals of uncooperative behaviour can be amalgamated into one general goal: to feel part of the group.

We are social beings and it is important to look at behaviour from a social context; in other words, everything we do can be understood in terms of relationships. Therefore, even if children get into trouble because of their uncooperative behaviour, they still enjoy a feeling of social significance; either from gaining attention, power, or retaliation. When this uncooperative behaviour works, they will naturally repeat it for as long as there is a payoff. In other words, if the child repeats a behaviour even though he knows it is wrong, you know he is doing it in order to achieve one of the four goals. Knowing this is crucial in dealing with the problem. The good news is, diagnosing uncooperative behaviour is an easy skill to learn.

There are three steps in diagnosing uncooperative behaviour:

STEP # 1 —What does the parent *feel* when the child is misbehaving?

STEP # 2 — What does the child *do* when the parent intervenes?

STEP # 3 — What are your *thoughts* when the child is misbehaving?

This three-step technique will be used in the diagnosis section following the discussion of each of the Four Goals.

The inappropriateness of undue attention

The child who wants undue attention feels significant only when she is the centre of attention. She enjoys it when people speak or notice her, even if they are yelling and upset. The usual cause of this problem is that the child received too much attention when very young, or only got attention when she acted up. When a young child gets showered with attention, she becomes used to having people talk to her and entertain her all the time. When this is not happening, even for a short time, she feels uncomfortable and attempts to regain the spotlight. The key payoff for this child is the interaction, and she will get it in sometimes phenomenally creative ways. Of course, uncooperative behaviour is one of the easiest ways to get attention (and keep in mind, that all children need and deserve a certain amount of attention. It is only *undue* attention when the needs of the situation don't call for it). For example, a child quickly learns that if she draws on the walls, her mom will come running.

Another form of attention getting that often isn't considered uncooperative behaviour involves the child who always does the right thing but who likes to point it out. This is called Constructive Attention Getting, and involves the least discouraged child of those trying to attain the four goals.

"Look Mommy. I tied my shoe!" Followed closely by "I love you mommy." Followed shortly by "Look. I just drew a picture for you." And another "Mommy. I love you."

Although this child is not doing anything wrong, his motivation is mistaken. He thinks the only time he counts is when someone is paying attention to him. This shows a dependency on others, as well as a mistaken way of fitting in with people. Deal with it by giving him less attention while encouraging him to be independent.

Of course, you must keep in mind that needing and wanting social interaction is natural. It is important, therefore, for the child to learn how to belong to the family through more constructive channels that result in closer relationships with family members.

Gloria is a single mom. She's also a bit of an overachiever who is raising three children while working at a full time job, and still somehow manages to keep the house spotless. Although she often feels overwhelmed by all of her work and responsibilities, Gloria doesn't let the children help clean up the house because she feels she can do it faster and better. Her hectic pace means she doesn't have time to spend with her children, even on weekends. Since Mom doesn't have enough time to spend with them, they resort to misbehaviour in order to get her attention. For instance, they fight with each other in order to draw her in, especially when she is on the phone.

"Stop fighting you two."

"But Mom. Shelly started it. She pulled my hair."

"Shelly, stop pulling your sister's hair."

"I did not pull her hair. She stole my doll."

Gloria puts her hand over the receiver. "Will you please stop fighting. I'm on the phone."

"But Mom. She won't leave me alone."

They also take advantage (unconsciously) of the fact that she likes to keep the house neat. They leave clothes scattered all over the house, eliciting endless reminders.

"Shelly, your socks are lying in the hall. Please pick them up."

"Sure Mom," comes the cheerful reply.

Shelly knows how to get her mom to notice her. As with most attention getters, she would rather receive negative attention than none at all. Gloria needs to put spending time with her children higher on her list of priorities. Because she is a single parent holding down a full time job, she is going to have to be creative about how she manages her time. One way would be to stop trying to keep the house clean by herself, and get the kids to help. This could be a way for children to make a contribution, while spending quality time with Mom. Gloria also needs to ignore their attention getting devices whenever she can. She can use logical consequences to prevent their recurrence. If they fight while she is on the phone, she could take the call upstairs in the privacy of her bedroom. This takes away the audience for the uncooperative behaviour, and therefore, there is no payoff. If the children leave belongings scattered over the house, a logical consequence would be to collect them in a big box and put them in an inconvenient place (instead of nagging). The main thing is to stop talking to them about the uncooperative behaviour. When the payoff is removed, the behaviour will stop. Always remember that the uncooperative behaviour might escalate at first (as the children redouble their efforts to attain their goal), but if Gloria stops the negative attention and steps up the positive attention, she should see a marked improvement.

Children as well as adults need attention. However, this attention should only be received when the situation is appropriate. Children who try to get attention by agitating others or being disruptive, only elicit annoyance and anger. It is also true that children who constantly need attention are generally unhappy, because they feel they have no place or sense of belonging unless constant attention is being paid to them. The reality is that they really do belong and have a place even though they are not receiving attention.

There are two reasons children strive for centre stage:

- They are pampered from the constant attention paid by adults and older siblings.
- They receive very little attention and crave connections to people.

Examples of uncooperative behaviour done for undue attention

- tattling
- shyness
- talking loudly
- dawdling
- asking a lot of questions
- talkativeness
- noisiness
- talking softly
- dressing inappropriately

Diagnosing the goal of undue attention:
(See page 56)

1. The parent feels annoyed and irritated while the child is trying to be the centre of attention.

2. When the parent intervenes, the uncooperative behaviour stops. This happens because the child has achieved her goal. Even a short verbal exchange with the parent can be enough.

3. The thoughts of the parent are along the lines of: "I wish she would leave me alone", or "what a pest!"

Strategies for handling undue attention

It's important to realize that acknowledging undue attention getting merely reinforces it. Any kind of acknowledgement — even negative — means the child has been successful at reaching his goal. By not paying attention you withhold all benefits. The trick is to only reinforce behaviour we find acceptable. If the child repeats the uncooperative behaviour, you can bet he is getting a payoff out of it. One of the best strategies is simply to ignore the behaviour.

There are three ways to ignore a child:

1. Remove yourself from the scene. Locking yourself in the bathroom or bedroom with a good book is a great way to do this. Without an audience, the behaviour will stop. Make sure you leave in silence. Even telling her why is giving her attention and letting her attain her goal.

2. Remove her from the scene. This is most effective for younger children. Without saying anything, take them by the hand and lead her outside, or to her room, or somewhere appropriate. Let her know she can come back and join the group when she is ready to act appropriately. This not only deprives her of her audience, but this consequence teaches her social interest as well.

3. Stay in the room but ignore the attention getting behaviour (mentally tune out). This is the hardest to do but is effective in instances when you can't leave the room or take the time to remove the child.

Believe it or not, if the behaviour gets worse *initially*, you are on the right track. In cases where she has been doing this for a long time, she is really just redoubling her efforts to get you to react the way you used to. Keep ignoring her and the behaviour will stop. When the negative behaviour does stop, that is the time to give her attention, in order to reinforce the socially acceptable behaviour. You should also look for times during the day when she is being cooperative or helpful, and point out to her how much you appreciate this.

Uncooperative behaviour for power

The child whose mistaken goal is power, feels significant when he can win the battle with the parent, get the parent to give into his demand, or not allow the parent to control him. Since he strives for power, he does not wish to appear weak. This child finds his place in the group by exhibiting his strength. This could involve outsmarting the parents with logic; stubbornly refusing to cooperate; or even physically overpowering them. He needs to be shown that his significance in the group realistically depends on his contributions: through his ideas and achievements. He must learn that he will not gain respect through his rebelliousness, nor does he need to because he is already a valued member of the group just by being who he is.

Struggling for power

As parents, we have to understand fully the concept of the power struggle and learn to develop techniques for dealing with it. We have to develop a new kind of authority, one that leads rather than dictates. Imposing our demands on children no longer works. Attempting to force children to do something often leads to power struggles. This is the child's way of fighting back. When children defy us, our prestige is threatened. But the most important aspect of a power struggle is that it is a no-win situation for both parties. Our challenge then, is to lead and stimulate them into cooperation. To head off power struggles, firmly decide what you the parent will do, not what you want to make the child do. For example, if your children refuse to keep their rooms clean, tell them "I will not be able to vacuum your room if your clothes and toys are not picked up."

The fact is, you really cannot force a child to do anything. Once we realize this we can turn to things like creativity, tact and a sense of humour to promote willingness on the part of the child. The old saying, "You can lead a horse to water but you can't make her drink" is very appropriate here.

There is a big difference between telling a 10 year old child that he must be in bed at 9 pm., and inviting him to help figure out how much sleep he needs and what time he should be in bed in order to get it.

Janice is an eight year old child who only feels significant when she wins. She battles her parents from morning until night, but the biggest problem is getting her to school in the morning. Although she normally runs everywhere, on school mornings she moves in slow motion. Her parents constantly glance at the clock and call out reminders: "Hurry up! You're going to be late! Come on — you've got to be out the door in five minutes!"

Meanwhile, Janice is upstairs, unable to find the right clothing match. She tries on four or five outfits and is still not happy. Her father comes and sees that she is not even dressed yet.

"Janice! What are you doing? We have to leave soon and you aren't dressed. You still have to eat breakfast."

"Stop rushing me. I won't go if you keep bugging me."

Dad is incensed. "You WILL go, and right now too."

Janice digs in her heels. "OK. I'm not going."

"If you don't get dressed and come downstairs right now, there will be no TV for a week."

"I don't care. I'm not going."

Janice has called Dad's bluff. She doesn't want to be told what to do. Every time she is told to hurry up or get dressed, she meets it with resistance. That's because she feels she is being overpowered when Dad gives her commands. Giving in makes her feel uncomfortably weak. When she defies him, she feels powerful and in control, especially when she can beat an adult at the game.

In truth, there is very little dad can do to get her to go to school. When threats don't work, what is left? But the reality is, Janice *wants* to go to school. She likes her teacher and all her friends are there. What Dad needs to do is extricate himself from the battle altogether, since this is a game he can't win. He should in particular not get mad, because every time he reacts in anger, Janice scores a victory. When she realizes he is at the end of his rope, she knows she has won the battle.

Dad should realize that it is Janice's responsibility to get to school on time. When Dad understands her unconscious goal, it makes it easier to not get angry. What also would help is for him to have a plan, so he doesn't get so out of control.

Dad can help Janice by giving her a clock and showing her when she has to leave to be at school on time. He should also refrain from giving her direct orders, and instead be firm about what *he* will do. For instance: "I know you are old enough now to handle getting to school on time yourself. I'm going to stay out of it. I'll be in the car and ready to take you to school at 8:30." The details of Janice getting herself out the door on time can be discussed at a neutral time (not in the heat of the moment), such as the family meeting.

If Janice decides not to go, Dad has to let the consequences of her tardiness happen at school (he should talk to the school about this).

Examples Of Misbehaviour For Power

- Defiance
- Yelling
- Temper tantrums
- Arguing
- Laziness
- Toilet training problems

Diagnosing The Goal Of Power:
(See Page 56)

l. The feeling that parents have when a child is battling them is one of anger and frustration.
2. When the child is corrected, he continues to do what he's doing in defiance of the request.

3. The thoughts of the parent are along the lines of: "I'll show her who is the boss," or "I'll *make* her do it."

Short term strategies for dealing with power

The main strategy is to avoid being drawn into the power struggle in the first place. If *you* win, the child feels weak because she has less power and is therefore more discouraged. If *she* wins, she feels more powerful and important and will continue to fight. The more power, the better she feels and the more she wants.

Learn to be firm. Tell her what you will do, not what she has to do: "I won't drive you if you act up in the car." As opposed to "Sit down and be quiet". If she won't go to bed, tell her: "I will be ready to read you a story and tuck you in at eight o'clock," as opposed to "I want you in bed by eight o'clock sharp and I mean it." Don't try to order her life for her but give her a lot of responsibility. Put her in a power position but in a way that benefits the group. Let her make pancakes for everyone, or look after the younger children. Respect her right to make decisions that affect herself and do not affect the rest of the family (her clothes, hair style, music etc.).

It takes two to fight, so withdraw from the conflict, especially from temper tantrums and verbal arguments. You only come back when the bad feelings have subsided. For one thing, this avoids damage to the relationship between parent and child. Remember, if you choose to withdraw, it is not a loss on your part (as many people think) because you have not conceded the point of contention. By withdrawing you have also prevented her from winning.

Another way to deal with power is to side-step the struggle. Work on the problem through good communication skills *(See*

Communication, Chapter 7). If your child wants to have a friend over to play but it's not convenient, instead of just saying no, suggest a different time. "How about if she comes over after noon when I'm not busy?" An even better way is to get her to find a solution. "I'm busy this morning, but I know it's important for you to have your friend over. When would be a better time for you to have her come?" Allow her to be creative in finding a solution. This teaches her to problem solve without feeling controlled.

The mistaken goal of revenge

The child seeks revenge when he believes that his parents do not like him and want to hurt him. These children often feel deeply hurt. They may have interpreted that the parents don't love them as much as the other siblings. They become extremely upset by the slightest rejection. These rejections can be real or imagined but whatever the case, the child feels unloved.

The desire to get even can follow hard on the heels of power struggles, when the parents use a lot of punishments in an attempt to win battles. The child then feels significant when he can get even by paying the parents back.

"You are a bad girl! You're going to get spanked again if you don't behave."

"I hate you! You're fat!"

Revenge doesn't have to be a prominent theme in a child's behaviour, but it can happen spontaneously.

The help we need to give a child who is seeking revenge is to convince him that he is loved and liked. This child needs affection and acceptance instead of verbal and physical abuse.

Sarah is the middle child in a family of three children. Her mother gives birth to a fourth child, but there are complications and she stays in the hospital an extra month. Her father is called away on business and the children are left with a nanny. After her mother comes home, Sarah begins to do uncharacteristically shocking things — she lights fires and disconnects the smoke alarm to increase the damage. She also begins to defecate in corners and write on the walls with crayons. When she goes to her aunt's house for the summer, this destructive behaviour stops abruptly, only to begin again when she goes home. It finally gets so bad, Sarah and her family have to seek professional help.

Sarah misunderstood what was going on when her mother and father temporarily disappeared from her life. She felt abandoned and hurt and wanted to hurt her parents back. It took a lot of work to get at the root of her motivation and rebuild her relationship with her parents.

Examples of uncooperative behaviour for revenge

- Vandalism
- Breaking toys
- Stealing
- Verbal or physical abuse
- Fighting
- Immoral behaviour

Diagnosing the goal of revenge:
(See page 56)

1. The parent feels hurt when the child is trying to get even with her.

2. When the child is corrected, he continues his behaviour until he feels he is successful in hurting the parent.

3. The thoughts of the parent are along the lines of: "I feel guilty because I don't like my child," or "How could she be so cruel and mean?"

Strategies for handling revenge

Don't punish her. Avoid giving logical consequences. If you have to, hold her until she stops the damaging behaviour. Tell her you love her but you won't let her hurt herself or anyone else. This lets her know you care about them while still stopping the damage.

Talk with the child a lot about her feelings. Use active listening techniques *(See Communication, Chapter 7)* to get to the bottom of the behaviour.

Give her a lot of physical affection. Spend time with her. Offer *unconditional love.*

(If the acts of revenge are serious and/or dangerous, the parents should seek outside professional help in rebuilding the relationship.)

The Mistaken Goal of Assumed Inadequacy

Of all the four goals this is often the most misunderstood because, unlike the other goals, inadequacy is not acted out by breaking rules or doing something wrong. It does not so much create anger in adults as it evokes concern. The child with this goal has come to the conclusion that there is no hope of being successful, either socially or academically. This could be because of a physical or developmental challenge (either real or perceived). The important point here is that it all has to do with the child's *perception* of himself; after all, some children with real challenges manage to overcome them and not feel inadequate. In any case, the child whose uncooperative behaviour goal is assumed inadequacy is an extremely discouraged child. Ironically, this can also be a result of extreme ambition, of either the parents or the child. If a child feels she has to excel and be better than others, she may give up when she sees that this may be impossible. Also, to this type of child, a mistake is nothing less than failure, and failure is too terrible to bear. That's because she feels that others will not like her or respect her if she fails.

The manifestation of this discouragement is that the child becomes passive and does not attempt to try. (Even if she *does* try, she fears that she will fail.) If you don't try, you can't fail. If the child wants to escape from the responsibility of trying, she has to convince others that she is hopeless, and that they should not expect anything from her. The goal of this child is to get people to leave her alone. She behaves in ways that prove her incompetency: she won't make even a small effort, she hangs back from participation, and is listless and withdrawn. This child needs a great deal of encouragement so that she is willing to take risks, which can only come about with improved self esteem.

> *Eleven year old Joey likes to stay at home and watch TV. He doesn't like to go out and play, or even go to school. When his parents try to encourage him to get out of the house and do something, he often says he has a stomach ache. Several trips to the doctors have found no physical reason for this. His reading and math skills are at a second or third grade level, far behind his sixth grade peers. Although he does poorly on intelligence tests, the feeling is that he has more capability than the tests show.*

Because he feels like such a failure in school, he keeps to himself. So much so that some of the children call him names. Whenever something is expected of him or he is asked to do something, he says he doesn't feel well, or that his favourite TV show is coming on, or that he doesn't like the kids who are playing baseball across the street. His parents have stopped making suggestions and leave him to himself. They explain the behaviour by saying he is just a quiet child who likes his TV, but deep down they are worried. He is pleasant at home and will help out when asked, but he seldom volunteers. His parents are thinking of a private school or a special program to help him get more involved in life.

Joey's discouragement has a lot to do with his younger brother who was born a year after him. Peter was an exceptional child who learned fast and had lots of friends. Over the years, the fact that Peter was the top of his class (not second but always first), was very important to Joey's parents. They always talked proudly about how Peter was the best athlete in the school, or the best speller in the city, and spent a lot of time with him. Everyone loved Peter, but paid less attention to the quiet Joey. Early on, Joey knew he had (psychologically) lost his place as the first born to his younger brother. He had been surpassed very early in life. There was no area where he could outperform Peter, so he simply gave up.

Examples Of Uncooperative Behaviour For Assumed Inadequacy

- Helplessness
- Withdrawal
- Over cautiousness
- An unwillingness to try
- Poor school performance

Diagnosing the goal of assumed inadequacy:

(See Page 56)

l. When a child is trying to impress the parents with his inadequacies and is successful in doing so, the parents develop a feeling of hopelessness and want to give up expecting anything from the child.

2. When the child is corrected, he remains passive and refuses to try.

3. The parents begin to lose faith in the child's abilities to achieve. The thought is: "Something is wrong with my child. I should take him to a doctor for tests."

Strategies for handling assumed inadequacy

Never let the child hang back and withdraw. Bring her into the group by saying things like: "Let's give it a try. I'm not going to give up on you. I'm going to help you because I believe in you. We'll work together to get through this."

Give her a lot of support and encouragement by focusing on her effort, not what she is producing. Show her where she has made improvements, even if it is just a very small improvement.

Children are uncooperative when they are discouraged. Their inappropriate behaviour (which is often unconscious), is always done in order to find significance. Your job as a parent is to diagnose this inappropriate behaviour and help them find better ways of fitting in.

- The Four Goals of Uncooperative Behaviour are:
    1. Undue Attention   3. Revenge
    2. Power   4. Assumed Inadequacy

- When handling inappropriate behaviour, the parent must think about the short term and long term strategies. The short term goal is to handle the behaviour at the moment. The long term goal is to overcome the cause so it won't happen again. You accomplish this by building up your child's self confidence and sense of social interest.

- Understanding why a child acts inappropriately is infinitely better than lecturing or punishment.

- Often the same behaviour can have different goals (i.e., whining can be for either undue attention or power).

- All uncooperative behaviour can be understood in terms of relationships, or the urge to belong. If a child is repeating a behaviour even though he knows it is wrong, you can bet he is being uncooperative.

- The Three Steps in Diagnosing Uncooperative Behaviour:
  1. What does the parent feel during the behaviour?
  2. What does the child do when the parent intervenes?
  3. What are your thoughts when the child is misbehaving?

- Undue Attention — This child only feels significant when others notice her. Of course wanting social interaction is natural, so parents must encourage constructive channels for this. The strategy is to not acknowledge the attention getting, but do pay attention when she acts appropriately. (The behaviour will get worse before it gets better — but that's how you know the strategy is working.)

- Power — This child only feels significant when he wins a battle with the parent. Your strategy is to not try to win. Lead but don't try to control him. Let him know what you will do, not what he has to do. Withdraw from the conflict. Put him in a position of power.

- Revenge — This child believes her parents don't like her. The strategy is, don't punish revengeful acts. Show the child she is loved, especially with physical affection. Talk about her feelings with her.

- Assumed Inadequacy — This child has come to the conclusion that he can't win. This is a very discouraged child. He is often passive and tries to convince others he is helpless. The strategy is to give him lots of encouragement and support. Don't let him withdraw or hold back.

Encouragement and discouragement

"Encouragement is more important than any other aspect of child raising. It is so important that the lack of it can be considered the basic cause for misbehaviour. *A misbehaving child is a discouraged child.*"

— *Rudolph Dreikurs, Children: The Challenge*

T he atmospheres shown in the previous chapter have discouraging elements. The opposite of the discouraging family atmosphere is the encouraging approach. The major difference is that in an encouraging atmosphere, the focus is on a child's strengths (what's "right" with the child, not on weaknesses or what's "wrong"). Even if you make a mistake in an encouraging family, you are encouraged to try again. Every effort is made to find something positive in the mistake itself. This gives courage to the child, the courage to take a chance and try something even if he doesn't know what the outcome will be. It gives him, in other words, the courage to fail.

What is encouragement?

Encouragement engenders a belief in yourself that you can do it, that you are lovable, and that your contribution is important. Some people are naturally encouraging. When you are in their company, you just feel good about yourself. Others need to learn how to be encouraging. It's a skill like any other, that can be broken down into component parts and learned. The first step in becoming an encouraging parent is to learn how to encourage yourself. You can do this by first accepting that nobody is perfect, and that we all make mistakes. If you lose your temper with your children, say to yourself: "That was ineffective. It may have let off steam, but it didn't help my child learn what it was I wanted to teach him. Next time I will be more effective." A lot of people that come into parenting classes feel bad about the way they have been parenting, too harsh, too permissive etc. They feel guilty, but guilt is a waste of time. Realize that the very fact that you are taking a parenting class or reading this book means you want to be a better parent, and start from there.

During their formative years, children look to their parents for their self image more than anyone else. You can encourage them by showing that you have faith in them. Give them opportunities to help and contribute to the well-being of the family. If something is a bit of a reach for them and they fail, let them know it was a good effort and that you know they will eventually succeed. All the while, remind yourself that mistakes are part of life and that failure is not a catastrophe unless we make it so.

The point to understand here is that it is important to work for *improvement,* rather than *perfection.* Try and set up expectations and goals the child can actually attain. Let your child know that his efforts are more important than the results: that it is more important to try than to succeed. After all, learning is a process in which we often fail at something but continue on until we get it right. Your job is to instill in your child the idea that it is all right to fail, that it is a part of learning.

We often underestimate children. This is so common that a parent will talk about a child to someone while the child is standing next to him, as if he were unable to comprehend. Having faith in our children lets them know that we trust them and have confidence in them. Many times children let us know what they are ready for. *"Mom, if we need milk, I'll go to the store and get it. I think I'm old enough now."* If we're not careful however, we can brush their eagerness under the rug and stifle their growth. *"That's OK. I have to go by the store anyway, so I'll get it."*

There are countless ways of showing your faith: in their choice of friends, their choice of extra curricular activities, and hobbies. Giving an allowance and letting them spend it as they wish demonstrates your faith in their ability to spend and save wisely. Also, by not interfering in fights with siblings and friends, you show that you have faith that they can solve their own problems.

Unconditional love is also encouraging. This means accepting a person exactly the way he is, not "If you comb your hair nicely", or "If you become popular at school". Sometimes parents want their child to be a certain way: to excel at sports, go out on lots of dates, or score well on school tests. It is discouraging when parents don't accept children for who they are. Let your children know that, even when they are doing things you don't like, you still love them. Affection and warmth demonstrate unconditional love better than words. Children love to be hugged. They like it when you walk with your arm around them, when you make eye contact, and the ritual of tucking them into bed and kissing them goodnight.

Humour can help. Laughing at adversity allows you to take setbacks in your stride. Humour is creative because it takes a situation (usually a painful one), and bends it out of shape. This is comforting because it helps you look at life in a different way. Any mistake can be funny. It always is in retrospect. When parents keep their sense of humour it can be used to break tension and prevent embarrassment.

Mistakes

One way to deal with "failure" is to separate "the deed from the doer". You do this by making a clear distinction between the action and the person who does it.

Four year old Ryan spills his wet paint set all over an upholstered chair. His dad says, "What's the matter with you? You are a sloppy boy."

This approach makes the mistake a problem with the child: the "doer". It's discouraging because the child interprets it as "there is something wrong with me." This doesn't make room for growth or change. The child might even start to believe he was born "sloppy".

Ryan spills his paint set on the chair. Dad says "Oh Oh. Looks like you have a problem there. Paint should never be used on this chair because it could ruin it. Let's clean it up and set up your paints over on the table."

This time Dad is focusing on the "deed". The child's sense of self has not been attacked. He won't feel as bad about making the mistake, while at the same time, understanding that it is possible to change and improve the situation.

An encouraging atmosphere is based on the principle that mistakes are not "bad" occurrences that need to be stamped out, but "good" things because they are learning opportunities that need only be taken advantage of. If a child makes a mistake, it proves he is willing to take a chance even though the outcome is imperfect. This shows the child has courage. Encourage him to do it again. The trick to encouragement is to find *something* the child did right in amongst all the things he did wrong. That's because you can't build on weaknesses, only on strengths.

Three year old Fatima surprises her parents one morning when she comes down stairs having dressed herself. Until now, Mom and Dad have always helped her select her clothes and then helped her get dressed. The surprise of seeing her dressed is quickly followed by suppressed grins. Fatima has chosen an outlandish combination of clothes, colours and prints. Her socks don't match, her shirt is on inside out, and she has on not one but two skirts. In short, she looks ridiculous — all except for the radiant look of achievement on her face. Mom and Dad cheerfully point out where she went wrong. "That was a nice try dear, but you should never wear polka dots with stripes, and I think one skirt would really be enough, don't you? Come on upstairs and I'll help you straighten yourself out."

The smile quickly fades from Fatima's face as she realizes she didn't do it perfectly. Her reaction is one of "I'm not very good at this. I guess I still need help. Maybe I should just let someone else do it for me."

A more encouraging approach would go something like this:

"Fatima, you dressed yourself. You went into the closet by yourself and picked out some clothes. I was down here making breakfast and you didn't need me to help you at all. You are really learning to take care of yourself now."

Fatima's parents have concentrated on her strengths and her positive intent: her courage to try something for the first time, as well as her sense of independence. And they didn't overblow the event. Some children like to hear a lot of praise about what they do. Others feel self conscious if you make too big a deal about it. Check out your child's reaction. Also, make a mental note of the polka dots and stripes and remember to find a time later to teach her how to match clothes. You can even make a game out of it by laying out her tops and bottoms with her and seeing if you can find which ones match.

Another roadblock is parental pride. Sometimes it's hard to let your child go out in public dressed the way she wants, mainly because you are worried about how it will reflect on you. You don't want people to think you aren't dressing your child properly. Tactful parents will point out to teachers and friends that: "Fatima dressed herself this morning."

We can be encouraging in everything we do. In fact, the difference between an encouraging and discouraging statement or action can be quite subtle. It could be, for example, the difference between looking at something a child has done and saying: "That's not bad, but if you did it this way, it would be perfect." (discouraging); and, "That looks great, you really seemed to enjoy doing it." (encouraging).

Essentially, encouragement makes us feel good about ourselves, even when we have made a mistake, and discouragement makes us feel that no matter what we do, we will never be good enough. Consequently, an encouraged person is convinced that she can find solutions to problems and cope with any predicament. A discouraged person lacks this kind of self confidence. Those of us with a strong sense of self worth can take any set-backs in our stride without feeling defeated. We pick ourselves up and are ready for the next challenge. But those without that strong sense of self tend to perceive every set-back as inevitable; as something they are powerless to stop. In short, the encouraged person feels able to handle life and the discouraged person does not.

Pampering

Pampering involves doing things for your child that she could do for herself. These kinds of parents always attempt to insulate their children from obstacles, frustrations and painful situations. They may suffer from a deep lack of trust, and don't believe their children can handle these things. Other parents take on all the responsibility because they feel that childhood should be a time of play. They can learn how to do things later. Ironically, they feel they are being especially good parents because they do so much for their children.

Pampering is discouraging because it robs the child of opportunities to feel useful. It can make the child doubt his capabilities. It also keeps him dependent. If someone is always doing things for you, you expect this to happen continuously. Then there is disappointment when this doesn't happen. He can also feel overwhelmed when others expect him to pitch in.

Megan is four and just stands there with her thumb in her mouth, waiting for her mother to put ketchup and mustard on her hotdog. The other children have all helped themselves, but this idea doesn't occur to her. Mother says sweetly: "What would you like me to put on your hot dog?" Megan points at the condiments.

At four years old, Megan is already resigned to other people taking care of her. She has not been encouraged to do things for herself, and is developing a passive and dependent nature.

Praise

It's important to make the subtle distinction between praise and encouragement. Praise evaluates the person and the outcome, while encouragement evaluates the deed and the effort put into it. Praise is a verbal reward. It can also be a label. Encouragement is more descriptive.

Here are some examples of praise:	Here are some examples of encouraging statements:
"What a smart kid you are — three A's on your report card."	"You're doing a good job of learning math, science and reading. You must enjoy those subjects a lot."
"You are so handsome (or so pretty)."	"You really put a lot of thought into your clothes today. Everything matches. Even your hair has been combed."
"You're a good worker."	"I appreciate the help you gave me."

Praise is problematic because it can only be used when the child has been successful. This can cause stress or anxiety because the child knows he won't get the praise next time if he doesn't pull it off. Encouragement, on the other hand, can be used at any time, even if the attempt is less than successful. Encouragement therefore, is more meaningful.

Going overboard with loads of enthusiasm can also be a problem, because it can be perceived as manipulation by some children. The same applies to telling other people about their accomplishments — "tell Grandma about how well you did on the potty". Some children like to do it and some don't. And pay close attention to how you phrase it. The difference between *"Tell* Grandma" and "Would you *like* to tell Grandma" is a subtle but nevertheless important distinction, changing it from a command to a request.

High expectations and perfectionism

Another parenting mistake to avoid is high expectations. This is encouragement pushed one step too far. When we push our children too much; when our expectations are too high for our children to attain, we set them up for failure or to at least see themselves as failures. Of course this does not mean that children should not be taught to do their best. Obviously we live in a competitive world where everyone must strive hard to succeed. But what has to be guarded against is the kind of mindless competition that is fostered so well by the "we're number 1!" ethos of sports, as well as the destructive and counterproductive competition that can easily be set up within families by comparing siblings to each other. ("Your brother can do that better than you. Let's see if you can beat him.").

Ultimately, standards that are too high send the message that so much of what we do is just not good enough.

Arthur is seven years old when he comes home with his first major report card. He has four A's, two B's and a C. He is proud of his As, and not overly worried about the other marks, so he is shocked when his parents tell him they were disappointed. They discussed the report card between them ahead of time and agreed on a strategy.

"We are very happy with the A's Arthur, but we know you can do better work in the other subjects," they tell him. "How come you got a C in spelling anyway? You couldn't have been studying for it very much. We think we should straighten out your schedule a bit so that you can concentrate better. Perhaps you should cut out extra curricular activities until you bring home a report card we can really be proud of."

"But that's not fair," Arthur protests. "I got four A's. Timmy Sullivan didn't get any A's and he isn't being punished. I'm not quitting baseball. You're mean. I won't do it. I hate my teacher for giving me low marks!"

His parents are disappointed at his reaction. They expected him to try harder, but remain firm. "You will do as we say. School work comes first. Now go to your room and get started this instant."

Arthur's parents focused on his weakest subjects and ignored his accomplishments. Saying you can do better is always discouraging, no matter how nicely you say it. Arthur originally felt pretty good about himself and enthusiastic about school. But now he's not sure. School is getting him into trouble. A little doubt now enters his mind: maybe he's not very good at school. On top of it all, he's angry at his teacher and his parents. Wanting to do school work is now the furthest thing from his mind.

A better reaction to Arthur's report would have gone like this:

> *"Wow! Four A's. You really seemed to enjoy the maths and sciences this term. And it says here your handwriting is getting better."*
>
> *Arthur's parents enthusiastically read through the entire report card together with him. They look at every mark and comment. Arthur himself points out his C in spelling. His dad says: "This C tells us that you need more work in this area. That's the good part about report cards. What can we do to help you improve your spelling?"*

Another common mistake parents make is to treat life as if it were a continuous classroom, where every single mistake has to be pointed out, criticized and corrected. It's hard, for instance, to not correct your child when he makes a mistake in verb tense "That's the *mostest* I ever saw.". But you must remember that children will eventually learn it themselves by hearing grownups say it. Constant criticism has the opposite effect of what is intended, and will slow down the learning process as the child feels less and less capable. If you find you are giving out one encouragement to every ten criticisms, you should reverse the ratio. Think about how you feel when you are criticized, and then feel how criticism must sting when you are a young child. Then think about how good it feels when someone sees through the mistakes you have made, and acknowledges your efforts.

REMEMBER: Encouragement is an ongoing process, so it's important to keep it up. One critical remark can undo a week's worth of encouraging ones. In an encouraging atmosphere, people feel free to be themselves because they don't have to be so careful about what they do or say.

Four year old Yvette is trying to pour milk over her morning cereal. Dad watches unobtrusively from behind his newspaper. The milk jug is a little big for her and she spills milk all over the table and on to the floor. She is aghast and quickly looks at Dad to see his reaction to the mess. "Did you have a little bit of a spill Yvette? That's all right. Lets clean it up and try it again. You get the cloth from the sink and I'll move the chairs back."

As they are cleaning up, Dad tells Yvette how happy he is that she is pouring the milk herself, and what a help it is when she tries to do things for herself.

After the mess is cleaned up, Dad suggests they pour the milk into a smaller jug, so it's not so heavy. He hands the smaller jug to Yvette and lets her pour. "I like the way you are holding the jug with two hands, Yvette. That should work." She still manages to spill a little milk on the table, but Dad says nothing and Yvette quickly cleans it up herself. Noting that she was still having trouble pouring, Dad waits until later that day and has a tea party with Yvette, where they practise pouring in a relaxed and entertaining atmosphere.

Instead of crying over spilled milk, Yvette's father downplayed the mess and paid attention to what she was doing right (holding the jug with two hands, and trying to pour the milk by herself in the first place). This lifts her self esteem at a time when she was feeling bad about herself. It gives her the courage to try it again. He also avoided correcting her pouring technique at the time of the spill, waiting until later to work on that. Sometimes, the worst time to teach a child something is when she has made a mistake and is feeling bad about it. It's important to put aside time for training, but the timing is important. Teach a child how to tie his shoelaces when everyone is in a calm and relaxed mood, not when he is late for the bus.

Finding fault is easy. Unfortunately, North America is a fault finding culture, so it comes naturally to us. Remember when your teacher marked all your wrong answers with big red X's? This reinforces our belief that if we point out what someone is doing wrong, he will correct it and not make the mistake again. But the truth is just the opposite — criticism lowers self esteem and actually makes it harder for children to improve. Of course, anyone with very high self esteem can handle a little criticism. Some children can take critical remarks in their stride. However, most children get more criticism than they can handle, and at that point it becomes discouraging.

Think how you would feel if someone yelled at you. Then think how your child feels when you yell at him.

Attributes Of A Well Rounded Child

- loves herself
- is able to have fun
- learns through mistakes
- doesn't blame others
- enjoys learning
- sees the positive in people
- accepts challenges
- does not have to be perfect
- cares about our environment
- has empathy for others
- doesn't worry unnecessarily
- takes responsibility for her choices
- continually moves towards self reliance
- enjoys life
- has courage
- is creative
- enjoys people
- loves others
- is not self critical
- is optimistic
- eats properly
- is not fearful
- is not afraid to try
- enjoys giving to others
- is interested in being healthy

Obstacles Leading To Low Self Esteem

- spoiling and pampering
- rejection
- overprotection
- criticism
- physical punishment
- feeling and showing pity
- unreasonably high expectations
- neglect
- lack of affection
- overly anxious
- finding faults
- name calling
- domination

An Encouraging Parent

- shows enthusiasm
- has confidence and faith in child

- recognizes efforts of child
- sees the humour in situations
- notices and remarks on child's improvement
- emphasizes child's strengths and assets

Making Encouraging "I" Statements To Your Child:

"I love you."

"I'm happy you are my child."

"I enjoy playing with you."

"I'm glad to see you."

"I'm so happy you're home."

"I missed you."

"I liked watching TV with you."

"I enjoy colouring with you."

"I hear that you were helpful, cooperative and did a good job."

"I appreciate your help, your ideas and your support."

"I love the colours you used in this picture."

"I like that idea."

"I like your hair, eyes, dress etc."

"I love your drawing, painting."

"I enjoy talking to you."

"I like being with you."

"I know you can do it."

Encouraging statements

Here are some examples of encouraging statements that can be used in almost any circumstances. Notice that some of them can even be used in negative situations. Also keep in mind that in order for it to work, you must have actual faith in your child. A preachy, patronizing tone will not work, even if the words are encouraging:

"You really seem to enjoy doing that."

"It would be a great help to me (us) if you could do this particular job."

"You are really getting much better at doing that."

"Don't give up. Keep trying."

"We like you, it's (a particular misbehaviour) that we don't like."

"I'm sure you can figure out a solution to this problem."

"I like the way you handled that."

"I know you want us to think you can't do that, but we think you can."

"You have to fix this. If you need help, you know where to find me."

Discouraging statements

Here are some examples of discouraging statements:

"Don't spill that."

"I think you could have done a better job of that. Your sister certainly could have."

"Oh no! You did it again."

"Here, let me do that for you."

"You're too young to do that."

"Don't get dirty."

"You could do that if you weren't so lazy."

"I thought I could trust you."

• Encouragement gives your child the courage to try — the courage to fail. Finding the positive aspects of a mistake and encouraging your child to try again are the hallmarks of this approach.

• Encouragement builds on the child's strengths and increases self esteem.

• Discouragement treats all mistakes as "bad", which makes the child fearful of making them and unwilling to try. Constant criticism, correction and judgement are the hallmarks of the discouraging approach.

• Discouragement concentrates on the child's weaknesses and lowers self esteem.

• You can encourage your children by:
  • Letting them know you have faith in them.
  • Working for improvement rather than perfection.
  • Treating all mistakes as learning opportunities.
  • Stressing that efforts are more important than results.
  • Stressing that it is more important to try than to succeed.
  • Using encouraging words.

• Praise is a verbal reward that evaluates the person.

• Encouragement evaluates the deed, not the doer.

- Pampering involves constantly doing for children what they could do for themselves, and sheltering them from all unpleasantness. This can lead to lack of self confidence.

- Having high expectations is encouragement pushed one step too far. It sets children up for failure.

- Humour is a good way to defuse discouraging situations.

- North America is a fault-finding culture. The belief is that if we point out mistakes and correct them, they won't happen again. But the opposite is often true — criticism can slow down the learning process by lowering self confidence.

The problems with punishment and reward

Punishment

In the autocratic parenting model of the past, punishment and reward were the accepted means of motivating children. It was the parent's responsibility to make a child comply with the rules. And in a limited way it worked, because when the punishment is severe enough, you can make the child do or stop doing something. Overall however, today's parents find that punishment doesn't seem to do the trick. First of all, corporal punishment is frowned upon in our society. Schools and other authority figures don't rely on it any more. And children have a sense that punishment is unfair in our democratic society. Even when punishment does seem to change behaviour for the moment, the child is usually complying out of fear. This fear can bring on anger, resentment and rebellion, which can harm the parent-child relationship. But worst of all, it is seldom successful at helping the child develop the internal control to behave well *on his own.* You want your child to behave because he knows it is the right thing to do and he wants to cooperate, not because he fears punishment. For one thing, the punishment won't always be around, but his sense of right and wrong (hopefully) will. In other words, what best bolsters our desires to improve ourselves is known as *intrinsic motivation* (while punishment and rewards are behaviour modification). The central idea of this approach is that the control of one's behaviour comes from within, rather than from someone else.

> *Six year old Jacob comes down late for breakfast and refuses to eat. Mom rolls her eyes. "Come on Jacob, that's not a good way to start the day. Now, eat your breakfast or you can't go out to play." Later, Jacob climbs up on the counter and tries to swipe some cookies. Mother gives his leg a quick slap and demands that he come down. He ignores her and begins stuffing his mouth with cookies until she grabs him and pulls him off the counter. He runs off to play outside with his friends. An hour later, he teases his younger brother, reducing him to tears. Mother gives him a "time out" for half an hour, and a stern lecture about getting along with others. She lets him back into the yard, but five minutes later he is again teasing his brother. This time his brother fights back and the kicking and hitting starts in earnest. Mom blows her top. "That's it," she says, grabbing him by the wrist. "You're going to your room right now young man, and for the rest of the afternoon."*

> *Upstairs, she hears Jacob throwing things around his room. The finale climax involves Jacob throwing a glass snow globe against the door, shattering it. Mom runs into the room and surveys the mess.*

"What am I going to do with you Jacob?" she
says helplessly. "You just wait until your
father gets home."

Mother and Jacob are caught in a never ending cycle of
power-punishment-revenge. Jacob's behaviour is saying, "I'll do
what I want and no one can control me." Mom has the mistaken
idea that through punishment she can break him down and
change him into the kind of person she wants him to be.
Unfortunately, the more she punishes, the stronger Jacob's
answer is: "If you have a right to banish me to my room, I have
the right to trash it."

Children are usually more tenacious and creative than
adults. They also don't feel as bound by social restraints as we
do: most parents wouldn't break something when they are
angry, for example, or hit someone to get revenge. The result is
that parents run out of ideas and energy. They don't know what
to do when the punishments don't work.

Often, these punishments go on day after day. You have to
ask yourself: If punishment works, why do I have to keep doing
it? The truth is, when we use power techniques in child rearing,
it only brings about rebellion, without instilling cooperation.

Rewards

"I need some help washing the windows. Who wants to
help," asks Mom. "What will you give us?", ask the
children.

The other side of this behaviour modification approach is
the idea of rewards: when children behave properly they are
given a treat or a special privilege for doing the right thing. In
the long run though, rewards don't work any better than
punishment, and for most of the same reasons.

The worst aspect of rewards is that children eventually begin to think, "I've got something coming to me" when they do the right thing. They will get angry when they don't get it. What's even worse is that the ante has to be increased every year. What starts out as package of candy or stickers when they are two years old, may grow into expensive bribes like clothes or even cars when they are teenagers. In other words, it is a dangerous precedent to set.

The reality is, it's not even necessary to give rewards. Children have a deeply rooted desire to do the right thing, and they enjoy the benefits of good behaviour the same way adults do. Rewards undermine this natural desire to cooperate, and substitute a "what's in it for me?" attitude. In addition, through the manipulation that is inherent in the giving of rewards, a child may feel controlled and overpowered. Resistance, rebelliousness and anger are often the outcome of this kind of control, just as they are with punishment.

We need to move on to a new child rearing technique; one that develops cooperative behaviour. In place of punishment and reward, we should use encouragement, as well as natural and logical consequences. This means moving parents out of the position of absolute power, and teaching them new methods of motivation. In this approach, the child is treated as a partner and a social equal. This is not to say that children are the same as adults, but that they are entitled to the same respect and dignity as adults. In other words, parents and children are in a partnership, and since the association is based on equality, punishment is not acceptable. You cannot punish or reward an equal in the same way that you would not punish or reward a friend.

Rewards often work quite well in the short term. Stickers, popsicles and money can get your children to do things that simply asking them won't. Lots of people think: "If it works, why not do it?" The answer is: Giving rewards can be short term expedient but long term foolish.

Roseanne's parents want her to practise the piano every day. Her teacher says she has potential, and it is her parents' dream to have a child that can play an instrument. But Roseanne isn't all that interested in playing the piano. She finds sitting down and practicing unsuited to her social, action-oriented personality. What she would rather do is play pop music and choreograph dance routines with her friends, or play soccer with her team. To entice her to play, her parents have drawn up a chart onto which she can stick on a star every time she practises. After 15 stars she gets to pick a toy. Roseanne practises for just long enough to wheedle a star out of her parents. There is no enthusiasm. Her progress is slow and her playing uninspired. But she does practise most days and her parents are satisfied that the rewards are helping.

Ask yourself what the real reasons are you would want your child to take music lessons. The answers would probably be: to learn to enjoy music, learn responsibility, and to stick with something. But Roseanne is not gaining any of these real benefits. Her parents have failed to find a way to get her genuinely interested in learning an instrument. They have managed to get her to practise, but in doing so they are also teaching her to dislike the piano. When the toys stop, so will her involvement in the piano, and probably the thought of learning any other instrument as well. Ironically, Roseanne might have taken up the piano on her own if her interest in pop music and choreography had been cultivated. Children often interpret rewards as controlling or as pressure, and this can nip anyone's interest in the bud. The real inspiration for playing an instrument should come from the pleasure it gives to the player and to other people.

> *Andrew's parents want him to learn to play the piano. Andrew is an active boy who would much rather play football than sit at a piano. His parents know he has a friend that is learning to play the guitar. They offer to rent an electronic keyboard and pay for lessons for Andrew, and suggest he and his friend could play together, perhaps even form a band and play for the family once a month. Obviously he will have to learn pieces already written, but they offer the possibility of he and his friend writing their own pieces as well. They even offer the garage as a place to practise. Excited by the possibilities, Andrew throws himself into his practicing.*

Rather than give rewards, Andrew's parents have inspired him by tapping into his goals and interests, making the motivation intrinsic.

Alternatives to punishment and reward

Abandoning the tools of punishment and reward is a big step, especially if you have used them for many years. In addition, you know you must still continue to discipline and guide your children. Children need limits: they need to know what is acceptable behaviour and what is not. The best way to provide these limits without having to rely on power techniques and manipulation is to use logical and natural consequences, along with constant encouragement.

S U M M A R Y

• In the now outmoded autocratic style of parenting, punishment and reward were the main ways of motivating children. Today's parents are more interested in "intrinsic motivation", which teaches children how to control their behaviour from within.

• Punishment and reward are short term expedient and long term foolish.

• Punishment can control behaviour, at least at the moment, but it can also cause resentment and rebellion and is useless in teaching cooperation.

• Rewards don't work any better than punishment, and for most of the same reasons. It makes children think they should always get something for doing the right thing. This "something" tends to increase as the child grows up. Rewards also undermine the child's natural inclination to be cooperative.

• Children want and need limits. The best way to establish these limits is with consequences and constant encouragement. In addition, treat your children as partners and equals. You can never punish or lecture to an equal.

Consequences

L ife is full of choices, and every one of our choices has a consequence. If we teach our children nothing else, we must teach them this. Some consequences happen naturally, and some can be arranged by the parents in order to teach their children life lessons. Whatever the source, consequences are the best way to teach a child. For one thing, the connection between the act and the consequence is crystal clear to children of almost any age. It's a lesson that really hits home and is remembered. For another, it keeps the parent out of the situation by putting the emphasis on the child's choice. This reduces the friction that punishment can cause in the parent-child relationship. When punishment is used as a correction, children frequently feel resentment towards the parent. Consequences are seen as being more "fair".

Consequences help children have a more realistic understanding of life's problems and give them an opportunity to use their creativity to alter their basic approach to these situations. In fact, consequences are the best learning tool human beings have to improve their social skills. They not only provide opportunities to learn through mistakes, but help children learn how to act in social groups as well. With logical consequences there is freedom to make choices. For these reasons, mastering the use of consequences is one of the keys to being an effective parent.

There are two kinds of consequences: Natural Consequences and Logical Consequences.

Natural consequences

A natural consequence is an unpleasant experience that nature imposes ("nature" is, after all, the root of "natural"). Life provides us with countless learning opportunities like this. If a bike is left out in the rain, it will become rusty and unusable. If we skip a meal, we are hungry. If we eat too much candy, we get sick. These kinds of cause-and-effect experiences teach our children responsibility, as well as giving them the reasons why some choices are better than others. With natural consequences, the parent doesn't interfere but lets nature take its course.

> *Every morning, it's a struggle to get four year old Pierre to wear a warm coat and mittens. His father knows that it is late fall and if Pierre goes for a walk or out to play, he will get cold — really cold! His main concern is that he will get sick. The word "pneumonia" keeps occurring to him. He pleads and begs and threatens but Pierre simply will not go out of the house with a coat and*

mittens. He even kicks and screams if Dad tries to force him into the clothes. Going outside has become a nightmare.

In desperation, Dad decides to withdraw from the power struggle and take a completely different tack, just to see what would happen if Pierre does go out dressed inappropriately. He tells Pierre that from now on, it's up to him to check the weather and decide what to wear. The next morning was especially chilly, and going to the park was an activity that Pierre wanted to do, so it was a good time for the experiment. Dad sticks his head out the door and says "Boy! It's nippy out there. I'm going to wear my warm coat."

Pierre goes out with him to the park wearing only a sweat shirt and jeans. After they get there, Pierre starts complaining that he's cold. Dad says, "OK. But first I want to see the deer pen. They've got a new baby deer."

Pierre is excited about seeing the fawn, but is so cold by now that he just wants to go. Dad agrees to take him home. By the time they get back, Pierre is even colder. He runs inside and sits on the hot air register. He then puts his coat on and asks to go back to the park, but Dad says no. "We had to come back early today because you were cold. Maybe tomorrow we can go back." Pierre argues that now he has his coat and won't be cold, but Dad stands firm.

The fact that Dad let his son get cold may be seen by some people as cruel or neglectful. The fact is, the child is not in any imminent danger of getting sick by going out on a chilly day. Obviously, if it were so cold it was life threatening, Dad would not let the natural consequences go so far. Nevertheless, the child has the right to make a choice, as well as the right to experience the consequences of that choice. Besides, until now all of Dad's threats and warnings about being cold fell on deaf ears. It wasn't until Dad took action by getting out of the way that Pierre began to understand *why* it is necessary to dress properly. If parents don't let their children experience these consequences, they will have difficulty developing good judgement.

There are usually different ways to handle specific problems with children. In the above scenario, Dad could have suggested that Pierre bring his jacket and put it on if he got cold. This gives him a choice and would appeal to some children.

Natural consequences are a great way to learn but as we have pointed out, they unfortunately *can't* be used when the child's choices are unsafe or unethical (playing near the top of the stairs, for example). For these instances, we must rely on logical consequences.

Logical consequences

A logical consequence is also an unpleasant experience that results directly from the child's actions. But unlike natural consequences, this logical outcome is arranged by the parents. For example, if a child is misbehaving in a restaurant, the parent takes her home before her meal is finished. She isn't taken to a restaurant again until she has learned to act properly. With this method, the connection between the misbehaviour and the unpleasant result is readily understood by the child. In this way, logical consequences are used as guidelines so that the child may understand the rules of social living. It is also used where a natural consequence can't be used because it is either too dangerous, immoral, impractical or infringes on the rights of others. For example, since it is too dangerous to let the child play in the street, we have to engineer a logical consequence to teach them about safety. If the child insists on playing in the street instead of on the sidewalk, the parent will keep him indoors until he is willing to stay off the street. Our purpose is to guide children to the realization that by not complying with the laws of nature and the laws of social living, difficulty and inconvenience will come about directly from their actions.

A consequence is different than a punishment. Logical consequences teach that there are *logical* connections between actions and results. Children then understand that consequences flow from their choices. Punishment, like a spanking, has no educational component. It is an arbitrary action imposed by the parent that is not closely enough connected to the behaviour. For example, a child choosing not to eat is sent to his room for the night. Being restricted to your room for not eating has no relationship to the deed of not eating. But when teenagers take the car without asking, they consequently can't use the car the next time they want to: *that* makes sense, logically.

The danger of punishment is that it can cause resentment, as well as discord in the parent-child relationship. Punishment becomes a battle between two people, i.e. my will against yours, whereas consequences place the emphasis on the child and the situation at hand. This allows the parent to provide guidance without producing animosity. Of course, not doing anything in the face of misbehaviour is as bad as using punishment.

Ten year old Chloe has been repeatedly warned to stop running near the flower bed, but she keeps doing it. Finally, one of her friends throws a beach ball that lands in the flowers. Chloe is an active child, and without thinking she runs into the flower bed and grabs the ball and runs out, leaving crushed and broken lilies in her wake. Mom and Dad are furious, but Chloe merely says she's sorry and runs off to play some more. Shaking their heads, her parents replant the flower bed and once more tell Chloe to stay away from them.

Chloe has become "parent deaf". Because their warnings to stay out of the flower bed have no consequence attached to them, she is able to simply tune them out. When she does make a mess, a simple "I'm sorry" always gets her off the hook.

Chloe's parents excuse her recklessness because they enjoy her spiritedness and don't want to spoil her fun. Unfortunately, Chloe is not learning how to govern her actions or to respect the property of others. Logical consequences would have helped. What her parents *should* have done was: 1) be firm in not letting her play near the flower bed once the rule was stated. If she persists, she should lose the privilege of playing in the yard until she is willing to stay away from the flowers; and: 2) once she broke the rule, she should have had to help restore the flower garden to the state it was in before she carelessly trampled it.

Sometimes parents are too quick to punish and then fix or replace whatever was broken themselves. But think of all the things that children could help repair. This also helps them learn how much effort goes into making the things of everyday life, such as gardens or clothing.

After borrowing her mom's shirt, twelve year old Dana ripped the sleeve. Afraid of her mother's reaction, she at first hid the shirt, hoping that no one would notice. Eventually, guilt drove her into showing Mother what she had done. Instead of being cross and then fixing it herself, Mom said: "Although I realize it was an accident, I feel upset when my borrowed clothes are ripped. Here's a needle and thread. Fix it as close to "good as new" as you can. If you have any trouble, I'll help you."

Dana was actually relieved that she wasn't going to be yelled at or punished. And fixing the shirt helped make amends to her mother, while increasing her sense of competence. Because of their lack of experience and judgement, children do make a lot of mistakes. So it's important to teach them at an early age that mistakes can be corrected, and that they can even learn something in the process.

When using consequences, it is important to understand the goals of the child's misbehaviour *(See The Four Goals of Uncooperative Behaviour, Chapter 3)*. If the child is seeking undue attention, logical consequences work well. On the other hand, children seeking power may view a logical consequence as just another aspect of the control the parents are trying to exert over them. If you are going to use a consequence and you know the goal of the misbehaviour is power, be sure to include the child in the discussion of what is to be done, always offering him choices.

Firmness means stating what <u>you</u> will do, not what the child will do.

Something else to keep in mind when using consequences, is to have faith in what children can accomplish through their own desire to grow and improve. Change can take time. It often won't happen overnight.

Amy, five, is fighting with her friends and being bossy. Consequently they don't want to play with her. As much as her mother would like to jump in and solve the problem herself by mediating, she bites her tongue and doesn't say anything. She has already told Amy many times that if she wants to have friends, she is going to have to share her toys and let the other children have a say in what games are played.

The next day, Amy is not having any fun by herself.

"Mom. I'm bored. I want to play with somebody. Can I invite Cindy over?"

"No honey. Yesterday, Cindy said she didn't want to play with you any more. Why don't you spend today thinking of ways you can play better with your friends. If you think you are ready to cooperate, we can call Cindy tomorrow and talk it over with her."

The consequence of being bored and lonely for the rest of the day is a valuable lesson for Amy. She already knows what she has to do in order to get along and have fun with her friends, because she has been told. Now it is only a question of how many times she must suffer the consequence of being lonely before she realizes that if she wants her own way, she won't have any friends. And, more importantly, having fun with other people for an afternoon is better than getting your own way for the moment. For this reason, consequences are a far better teacher about life's difficulties than parental lectures. Children can fight back when a parent tries to teach them a lesson about life, but they can't fight back against natural and logical consequences. It is hard to watch your child suffer rejection, but letting them experience it is the best way to prevent more suffering in the future.

Words — to use them or not

Sometimes a logical consequence happens spontaneously. Your three year old is about to hit your five month old with a heavy toy and you quickly scoop the toy away. The consequence is that the child can't use the toy. There is no time to discuss the problem, because some situations call for immediate action.

At other times, however, you have to use words to explain the consequences. For example, if your children are misbehaving at the mall, you tell them (in a firm and friendly voice) "I will have to take you home now. When you learn not to fight with each other and bug me for toys I'll bring you back." Nothing else need be said by the parent: the few words and the action that follows are enough. Moralizing or excessive talking will backfire. Remember, at this point it is easy for dialogue to regress into bickering or undue attention getting. The rule of thumb is to state *what you will do* and no more.

If you are having an ongoing problem, you sometimes have to sit down at a neutral time and work it out with your child. For example, your child has been repeatedly rude and disrespectful to you. Through discussion, you explain that you are not willing to be in the room with someone who is treating you that way. The next time it happens, the child will have to leave the room and be alone until he is ready to behave respectfully. From now on the child knows what to expect from this kind of misbehaviour. To reinforce this, it is important to be both consistent and act quickly so that the misbehaviour does not go on a long time.

> *The Wongs are having a family get together. Their three year old, Kirk, is up much later than usual and over excited by all the people and the attention he is getting. He starts running and screaming through the crowded dining room. At first everyone laughs at his antics. But soon he is banging into people and knocking over glasses on the buffet. The room is too small and too crowded to let this behaviour continue. But when Dad asks him to stop, Kirk laughs, pulls away and runs off even faster.*

His Dad goes after him. Kirk is even happier — now he has Dad involved in a chasing game. Dad sees that Kirk is not listening to him; he is obviously tired and needs to go to bed. He picks Kirk up — despite his loud protests and struggling — and takes him to his room and puts him to bed.

The consequence of Kirk not being able to behave at the party was that he had to be removed from the room and be put to bed. If he had done the same thing earlier in the afternoon, he could have been given a choice: either stop the running and screaming, or go out into the backyard where it wouldn't bother anyone.

Be creative

At first, it may be hard to come up with a logical consequence for every misbehaviour. It takes time and creativity to begin thinking this way. Start by asking yourself "What would happen if I didn't intervene?" This helps point you in the right direction.

Three and a half year old Juan refuses to get dressed in the morning, even though he has shown that he can easily dress himself when he feels like it. It's not so much that he fights, but that he dawdles and gets distracted. Mom lays out his clothes for him and comes back five minutes later, only to find Juan playing with his colouring book. She knows she hasn't got much time before he has to be at day care. Because of this, Juan has her complete attention as she wheedles, begs and tries to bribe him into getting dressed.

"Come on, Juan, lets get dressed. OK?"

Juan ignores her and starts crawling under the bed.

"Please Juan. We're going to be late. If you get dressed, I'll buy you a toy."

He brightens at the prospect of a toy, and starts pulling on his pants. "I really love you mommy."

"I love you too, Juan. But please move a little faster, we're going to be late."

Soon, Juan goes limp and just lays on the bed. In desperation, Mom finishes dressing him herself and carries him out to the car.

"That's the last time I'm going to dress you, Juan. Tomorrow you can do it yourself. I know you can do it because your teacher told me you dress yourself at recess."

The next day, however, the scene of Juan's uncooperative behaviour is repeated, and once again Mom has to dress him.

In the above example, if Mom hadn't intervened Juan would not have got dressed. But, except for a few difficult tasks like tying his shoe laces, Juan *can* dress himself. He doesn't do it because he enjoys the service and attention he gets from Mom (the goal of undue attention). Because Mom is taking all the responsibility for getting him dressed and out the door on time, he doesn't have to learn to take responsibility for himself. The solution is to find a way to shift the consequences of not dressing and of being late onto Juan's shoulders.

After taking a parenting course, Juan's Mom decides to let him experience a logical consequence of dawdling. She tells the day care not to be surprised if Juan shows up in his pajamas. Then, as she is tucking him in the night before, she tells him that if he decides not to get dressed in the morning, she will take him to school in his pajamas.

The next morning, she lays out his clothes like before. "It's time to get dressed, Juan. I'll be down stairs getting breakfast so we can leave as soon as you eat."

Ten minutes later, Mom calls up (in a very friendly voice): "Juan. Breakfast is ready."

Juan calls down: "I'm not dressed yet."

Mom ignores this and sits down to her breakfast. When she's finished, she clears the table and puts everything away. Still no Juan. Now it's time to leave. She goes upstairs and finds Juan, still not dressed and playing with his hamster. "It's time to go Juan. I'll put all your clothes in a bag and you can dress yourself at school."

"But I'm hungry," he cries.

"Sorry Juan. Breakfast is over. You can eat some bread in the car."

"But I can't go in my pajamas. I'll get dressed now."

"No. We don't have time. We have to leave right now."

Juan starts to cry, as Mom picks him up and takes him to the car.

At school, the other kids gather around him and ask him why he's still in his pajamas. Juan darts into the bathroom and quickly gets dressed. Nothing more about the incident is said to Juan by either his mother or the teacher. Juan knows what has happened. He was embarrassed at school, plus he didn't get the kind of breakfast he likes.

The next morning, Mom lays out the clothes. Juan dawdles for a little while but Mom doesn't come to hurry him up. Instead, she calls out that breakfast is ready. Soon, an out of breath Juan runs down the stairs shouting, "I'm dressed!"

That morning they were on time for school, but a week later he again tested Mom by fooling around and not getting dressed. Once again, he missed breakfast and showed up at school in his pajamas. After school, he announced to his mother: "I'm going to get dressed real fast from now on."

Mom's use of logical consequences demonstrated to Juan that she would no longer be in his service. If he wanted to have a good breakfast and avoid being embarrassed at school, he would have to take care of it himself. By doing things for Juan that he could do himself, it robbed him of the opportunity to learn to do things on his own, and to feel proud of his own growth.

Remember that there is often more than one solution to any given problem. In the above scenario, Mom could have worked on setting up a routine so that Juan would get used to doing the same thing every morning. He would know that breakfast would be ready as soon as he got dressed, and if he didn't get dressed on time, no breakfast. For some children, this in itself might do the trick.

Here are some examples of Natural Consequences:
- If a child chooses not to eat, she's hungry.
- If a child chooses not to dress properly, he's cold.
- If a child doesn't watch where she's going, she can bang her shin.

- If a child spends all his allowance right away, he won't have enough for what he needs later.
- If a child doesn't get enough rest, she will be exhausted.

The following are examples of Logical Consequences arranged by the parents:

- If a child is not on time, he misses out on fun.
- If a child doesn't clean up her room, her parents won't come into her room to tuck her in.
- If a child is making noise in the house, he will be asked to go outside where it won't bother anyone.
- If a child is being rude in the restaurant, she has to leave.

Here are some more examples of misbehaviour and their appropriate logical consequences:

If the child breaks something:

- If it is something that belongs to the child, it is not replaced.
- If it belongs to someone else she must fix it, replace it by using her allowance money, or give up one of her own.

If the child wants to argue:

- The child is asked to leave and may return only when ready to discuss the problem calmly.
- The parent can leave the scene and the child can't be with the parent.
- The child is brought back home if out in public.

If the child is demanding:

- The child does not receive what she wanted (the TV turned on, food, a game to start, etc.).
- The child is asked to leave the room until he can ask politely.
- The parents leave the room until the child can ask politely.

If the child dawdles:

- The child is late and misses out on the activity.
- A baby sitter can be hired and the child misses out on a family outing.
- The child is late for school and faces the school's own consequences for tardiness.
- If he is dawdling at the dinner table, his food is removed when everyone has finished eating and the child has to wait for the next meal.
- If the child is delaying going to bed, he misses out on story time.

If the child doesn't put things away:

- Toys are removed until the child is willing to take responsibility.
- Clothes and other belongings left around the house are placed in a box in an inconvenient place like the basement.
- If dirty clothes are not put in the hamper, they are not washed.

If the child refuses to do chores:

- If the table is not set, dinner cannot be served.

- If the laundry is not done, the child (and his siblings) must wear dirty clothes.
- If the kitchen counter is left messy, the parents can't cook dinner.
- If a pet is not taken care of, it is given away to a better owner (of course, children under 12 should not be expected to assume full responsibility for an animal).
- If the garbage isn't taken out, it can be put in the child's room until it is.
- The parents go on strike and nothing gets done in the household (this is only done in an extreme case where nothing else works).

The positive aspects of logical consequences are:

- It is a way for the parents to teach the child about life.
- Children come to see that their decisions and actions have very real outcomes that cannot be avoided.
- If done properly, the relationship between the parents and the child does not suffer, as it does when punishment is used to teach the lesson.
- Consequences help a child's self esteem because it is essentially self taught.
- It focuses on the child's choices but not on the child herself.
- Children will see the fairness of a logical consequence more than punishment.

For logical consequences to work, the following rules are needed:

1. The consequence must be related to the behaviour.
2. Choices must be given whenever possible.
3. The tone of voice must be friendly.

4. Do not use when the child is engaged in a power struggle.

5. Always be sure the child knows there will be a second chance to improve.

6. The parent's attitude must be one of teaching. This will be easier if you don't let your ego or your emotions get involved in the problem. If you feel yourself getting angry, it is not a good time to try and arrange logical consequences.

Punishment is different from consequences in the following ways:

- It may teach the child not to get caught, but not the necessary lesson of why her behaviour is not acceptable.
- It enforces the will of the parent over the child.
- Punishment can be used to retaliate rather than correct.
- The child may harbour resentment against the parent because she interprets the punishment as: "unfair", "you're all against me", "you're mean", or "you don't love me".
- It expresses the power of personal authority, rather than helping the child understand the need for cooperation.
- It is not related enough to the misbehaviour. For example, there is no connection between depriving the child of TV and the fact that he didn't eat his dinner.
- Often it is done in anger.
- In some cases it may motivate the child to gain power over others later in life.

- Every action and every choice we make has a consequence. These consequences are great ways for parents to teach their children the lessons of life.

- Natural Consequences: Some consequences are provided by nature, i.e.; if you leave your bike out in the rain it will get rusty. If you don't wear a coat you will get cold.

- Logical Consequences: Some consequences are provided by the parent (especially if the natural consequences are too dangerous or unethical), i.e.; if the child deliberately breaks something, he must replace it out of his allowance.

- Consequences are different than punishment. With consequences, there is a logical connection between the act and the consequence. Punishment is an arbitrary act that the child learns nothing from.

- Punishment can cause resentment and rebellion, whereas consequences place the emphasis on the child and the situation at hand.

- Some consequences are imposed at the moment of the misbehaviour in order to prevent damage or injury (taking a ball away before it is thrown through a window). If there is time, the parents explain to the child — in as few words as possible — what he is doing and why.

- When using consequences, it is important to act quickly and be consistent.

Communication

Learning how to communicate in a respectful manner is critical for anyone wanting to have a close relationship with a child. Respect for a child means listening to him and taking what he says seriously. This lets him know that we care about him. When talking to children, talk with the same amount of respect you would give to one of your friends. This means accepting what the other person says, even though you may not necessarily agree with it.

Good communication helps people form healthy relationships by doing everything from solving problems and developing empathy, to learning about the world and about themselves.

Not all communication is effective. For instance, we have all experienced these common obstacles to communication:

- monologues
- orders and commands
- warnings
- moralizing
- lecturing
- blaming

- demands
- directing
- threatening
- advising
- criticizing
- ridiculing

Kweku, an avid jigsaw puzzler, is upset because he keeps losing the pieces to his puzzles. He goes to his dad to complain.

His dad's reaction is: "You know what? It's your fault because you're unorganized. You're five years old now — you should be putting all of the pieces to your puzzle in the same box every time you're through playing with it. If you can't learn to take care of your toys, maybe you shouldn't be playing with them."

Kweku frowns and goes off to play with something else.

In the above example, there are numerous obstacles to effective communication. Although Dad came up with the obvious solution, the point never hit home because of the way it was communicated. Kweku feels slightly stupid and a little resentful. Also, because he received a lecture, Kweku is not as likely to come to Dad with his problems in the future. Although it was a small incident, Dad's response succeeded in quickly shutting down the communication process. It was totally one sided instead of the two-way dialogue communication is supposed to be. This is a very common way parents talk to children; they give the solution and then berate the child for not coming up with it himself. Or they attach blame. But it doesn't have to be that way. Here is how Kweku's dad *could* have handled the problem.

> Kweku tells his dad about the missing pieces of his puzzle. His dad says: "It sounds like you're getting frustrated because you can't put your puzzle together."

> Kweku nods his head.

> Dad continues: "Lets figure out what needs to be done to help you get organized. Why don't we search together for the pieces and put what we find in the puzzle box?"

> Once Kweku and his dad collect all the pieces, Dad says: "Now lets talk about how you can keep from losing your pieces. What do you think we could do?"

> "Why can't you and Mom do it for me?"

> "I think your mom and I would be too busy to look after your toys for you. I bet if we could figure out a way to organize your puzzle pieces, you could keep track of them yourself. How about that?"

> Kweku goes along with the suggestion. Dad asks again for ideas, but Kweku draws a blank, so Dad says: "How about if we have a table that is only used for your puzzles? That way they will always be in the same spot. We can even put up a shelf so that you can always put your puzzles in a safe place. What would be a good rule to make when you're through playing with your puzzles?"

> "The rule should be that I put my puzzles away on the shelf," says a beaming Kweku.

Dad listened to the problem and repeated it back just to make sure it was understood. He didn't ridicule or lecture Kweku, but patiently helped Kweku come up with the solution. He also encouraged him to share his concerns and to be independent.

The results of poor communication

Pretend for a moment that you are a child that is constantly exposed to poor communication methods. The following are ways that you could be expected to respond:

- Merely say what the authority figure expects you to say;
- Avoid expressing your feelings;
- Always ask for permission;
- Do not express your thoughts;
- Keep your wants and needs to yourself;
- Play stupid;
- Do not question or disagree;
- Act as if everything is OK.

People who practise effective communication skills avoid these kinds of behaviour. That's why you should always listen to each other in an empathetic, non-judgemental way. Try to always keep your voice friendly and your mind open. Always attempt to reveal as much about yourself as you are learning about others. And remember, to have truly open communication you must allow for disagreements, for the expression of both positive and negative feelings without fear.

One of the most important concepts for good communication is that of social equality. In our relationships (except for friends), we have been raised to relate to people as either being above or below ourselves. This makes it difficult to communicate with people we consider to be either in authority or subordinate to us. But communicating with people on a mutually respectful level requires skills most of us don't have. Is it any wonder then that there are serious problems in marriages, or the relationships between parents and children, children and their friends, and even between countries? If we are going to learn to communicate more effectively, what better place to start then with our own children?

Sometimes children find it hard to talk to adults. How often, for instance, have you asked your child what he did at school today, only to have him say, "Nothing"? One reason is that these questions smack of control; "I ask you a question and now you have to answer it." Or maybe the timing is wrong because he wants to go out and play. But often it is because kids live in the present and what they did at school was in the past. Parents have to learn how to sometimes think like a child and not like an adult. Sometimes instead of a question, a better opening is telling them what you did that day. Or you could wait for them to bring up a topic, like: "Brittany's hat got thrown up on the roof today." Use this as an opener to get them talking about what happened in school.

Other than the above exceptions, the rules for communicating with children are the same as with anyone else. The following are the skills that need to be practised by parents in order to become effective communicators:

Listening

The first step to good communication is listening. Sometimes parents are better at talking then listening. Often communication is thought of as a "talking" skill, but a large part of good communication is listening: active listening. Active listening requires both verbal and non-verbal skills. The idea is to try and understand what the other person is going through by being empathetic; to make sure we understand the content of what he is *saying*, as well as what he is *feeling*.

To be a good listener, one has to remain silent while the other person is speaking and maintain good eye contact. In order to let the person (a child or an adult) know we understand the feeling and the content behind what is said, we have to learn to summarize the content for the speaker, as well as to reflect on the speaker's feelings. This is called reflective listening and involves repeating back what the child has just told you. For example, the child says: "I hate school. My teacher yelled at me in front of the class!" You might say back: "You seem very upset because you got in trouble today." If the understanding is not clear, then the child can rephrase it. "No, I'm upset because I got yelled at in front of the other kids." This improves communication skills and helps us to become more in tune with the child's thoughts.

Good listening skills

Being a good listener is one of the most unappreciated of the social skills. The benefits of good listening skills are:

- Children are more willing to talk;
- Helps children defuse strong negative feelings;
- Children feel you care about them;
- Helps children to realize that feelings are good and can be used constructively;
- Improves relationships — resulting in cooperative behaviour;
- It is a form of encouragement;
- It demonstrates unconditional acceptance;
- Helps make problem solving easier;
- Keeps the problem the responsibility of the child;
- Helps develop better self esteem;

- Helps the child become a good listener;
- Helps children label their emotions and therefore, understand them better.

Requirements parents must have for good listening skills:

- A deep sense of trust in their children's ability to solve their own problems;
- An acceptance of children's feelings;
- The strong desire by the parents to help their children with their problems;
- The ability to respect the confidentiality of their child's conversations.

Two Kinds of Listening Skills:

1. Passive Listening

Allow the child to talk freely. Don't interrupt, but respond only with encouraging sounds and gestures, such as "uh, huh's" and nodding of the head. Besides eliminating negative comments, remaining silent is itself an indication that you accept what the child is saying. This can only encourage a child to continue talking about what is bothering him. The only problem with passive listening is that the child might not feel fully understood because you are not giving him feedback. If you feel this is a problem, switch to active listening.

2. Active Listening

This involves taking what the child has just said and saying it back to her in a different way. This lets her know what you think she is saying. It also gives her a chance to correct you. You use active listening when you think the child is undergoing an emotional feeling that is stronger than usual.

Lisa, who is ten, doesn't want to go to her Saturday morning swimming class. "I don't want to go to swimming any more," she announces as it is time to go.

"Why not? You used to love swimming class," says Mom.

"The coach is always telling Betty and Veronica how great they are, but he never says anything nice to me. They win most of the races and I don't win anything. I just don't think I'm very good at swimming any more."

Mom nods and says "Uh huh."

"And the kids aren't as friendly to me as they are to Betty and Veronica because they win all the races. I think they have become stuck up since they have won so much. They used to be my best friends, but now they think they're too good for me."

Lisa starts to cry.

"Lets see if I understand why you don't want to go to swimming any more," says Mom. "The coach has been ignoring you and has been paying a lot more attention to Betty and Veronica who have been winning a lot of races. And Betty and Veronica, who used to be your best friends, have made friendships with other kids. It sounds like you're feeling hurt and deserted."

"I'm not hurt, I'm angry at them because they make me feel left out. I never did that to them."

Active listening can also be used when the child is excited or happy.

Four your old Claire just got a new puppy. At day care, she tells her teacher all about her new pet. "He's the cutest little yellow puppy," she says. "Her name is Bowser and my parents let her sleep with me."

"You sound so happy," her teacher says. "It must be fun to have a puppy to play with and company at night."

"Yes, and I won't be lonely any more. All my friends have brothers and sisters, but I don't. Now I have somebody to play with."

Some active listening phrases are:

"What I hear you saying is _____."

"It sounds like you are feeling _____."

"Let me see if I got that right...."

Some encouraging responses to a child's dialogue could be:

"You're saying _____."

"In other words_____."

When you do this you are paraphrasing, or rephrasing. This involves hearing what a person says and then saying it back to her in your own words. This is a way of letting the person know you are listening to her, but it also lets her correct you if you got it wrong. For one thing, it is much better than the usual useless catch phrase: "I know what you mean."

Example problem

"I had a hard day at work. I didn't get all my work done and my boss asked me to stay late. I still had to pick up the kids and make dinner and everything else I have to do. On top of it all, I feel that my boss is inconsiderate of my needs."

You can rephrase this statement to include a summation of the content, as well as what you think the feeling is behind what the person is saying:

"It sounds like you feel overwhelmed with the amount of work and responsibility on your shoulders, and also really angry that your boss doesn't care about that."

You can paraphrase the content of what your child is saying in your own words by making a brief statement about what the child was experiencing. In order to do this, the parent needs to pay attention to the 5 W's.

For instance, if your child wants to talk about a fight he had during recess, you would ask:

1. Who or what was involved? (Your child and his friend)
2. What did they do? (They had a fight.)
3. Why or how did they do it? (Because a friend called him a name.)
4. When did they do it? (During recess)
5. Where did it happen? (On the school yard)

The most important part, however, is to reflect the feeling that the child experienced. Ask yourself, "How would I feel if this happened to me?" After coming up with your own feeling, the parent reflects it back to the child by saying something like:

"It sounds like you feel hurt (the emotion) because your friend was mean to you (the content)."

Paraphrasing also helps you and the child know that you have understood what has been said. Asking questions not only lets you find out more about a situation, but lets the child know you are interested as well.

Open and closed questions

There are two kinds of questions: open and closed. Closed questions are less effective and may shut off the communication process. A closed question looks for specific facts. ("What time was this when it happened?") Closed questions are ineffective because the child might find it irrelevant and may interpret it as an attempt by the parent to control the direction of the conversation.

> *"Bobby never wants to talk to me," Mom is telling a close friend. "He only gives me one word answers and then walks away. Here he comes now. Watch."*
>
> *"Hi Bobby. Where were you just now?"*
>
> *"Nowhere."*
>
> *"You must have been somewhere. Were you being a good boy?"*
>
> *"Sure."*
>
> *"Who were you playing with?"*
>
> *"Nobody."*
>
> *"Do you want something to eat?"*
>
> *"No."*

Open ended questions attempt to discover the child's view. They may ask for his feelings about the situation: "How do you feel about it?" "Could you tell me more about_____?" This usually requires more than a one word answer.

Sam walks in to the kitchen. "Hi Sam," his mother says. "I drove by your school at recess and saw you and your friends playing a game. I'd love to know what kind of a game it was. It looked like fun."

" It was called Red Rover."

"How does Red Rover work?"

"Well, you pick teams and one team links hands and says something like: 'Red Rover, Red Rover, we want Sam to come over.' and the other team sends me running at it, trying to break through. It's fun. Our team won."

The "I" message.

An "I" message indicates that you are taking responsibility for ownership of the emotions caused by the problem. A "You" message, on the other hand, attaches blame to the problem.

"I" messages are more effective in resolving the problem while "you" messages can lead to power struggles, guilt feelings and the lowering of your child's self esteem.

Here Is A Typical "I" Message:

"I feel frightened when you wander away when we are in a store, because you may get lost."

Notice that there are three distinct parts to an "I" message. One is a statement about how you are feeling ("I feel frightened."). The second is a statement of the problem you are experiencing ("When you wander away in the store..."). A third is a statement of the consequence of the child's behaviour ("you may get lost").

The Three Aspects Of The Message Are:

"I feel_____ when you _____
because_____."

Another way of communicating a problem is to state the problem while leaving out the "feeling" aspect, such as:

"I can't wash the dishes when the dishes are not cleared from the table."

The important thing to remember is who the problem belongs to. If the problem belongs to the parent, for example, the parent must take responsibility for it. It is also essential that the parent does not blame the child:

"You make me very upset when you don't clear the table."

Blaming children can lead to power struggles, which gives them the opportunity to gain a victory over their parent and therefore, encourages them to repeat the unacceptable behaviour. To avoid blame, put it this way:

"I feel very upset when the table isn't cleared."

Communication processes can also be non-verbal. Our facial expressions and tone of voice communicate more than you might think. For instance, parents may be condescending, use baby talk, or speak as if the children are unable to understand normal conversation. Children are very aware of being talked down to. Always talk to children as equals. This, of course, is a matter of tone, not content; you wouldn't talk to children about adult themes, for example.

When we criticize children or find fault with what they think, they soon become closed to adults and hide their true thoughts and feelings. We do not always have to tell children their ideas are wrong if we disagree with what they are saying. We have to recognize there are more points of view than our own. Stress that their ideas and viewpoints are important.

Moralizing to children is another method of creating distance between parents and children.

> *"I don't want to invite Marty to my party. I don't like him any more."*

> *"Oh, you must invite him. You can't not invite someone just because you had a little spat."*

Instead, ask the child questions in order to help him and you come up with solutions to problems. For example:

> *"How do you think your friend will feel if you don't invite him to your party?"*

If you try to solve problems alone, without the children, you lose the opportunity to influence their behaviour. The best way to solve problems is by talking and exploring together.

Anger is one of the least admired emotions. That's because it is destructive when it gets out of hand. But anger is also an essential human tool. It is the emotional equivalent of pain — it lets us know something is wrong. Anger is useful in problem solving because it helps us move towards finding a solution. From a parenting perspective, it lets our children know that what they are doing is unacceptable. The key to anger is to understand what it is and to express it properly.

Contrary to popular belief, you are always in control of your anger. If you don't believe that, ask yourself how many times you have been extremely angry about something, but can pick up the phone when it rings and talk quite pleasantly and coherently. Usually, you let yourself become very angry because you want *immediate* results. Yelling at someone is about power, but you can let a child know that you are angry just by the inflection of your voice, without resorting to screaming. It is all a matter of degree. When you use your anger to intimidate and cause fear, you have gone too far. But on the other hand, you do have to let your children know that certain kinds of behaviour make people angry. The best way to do this is to express your own anger in a firm, serious voice. If someone has broken a window through sheer carelessness, let him know how you feel about it. Tell him why you are angry, that it costs time and money to fix a broken window. *(See Problem Solving, Chapter 10)*

When parents yell all the time, their children can quickly become immune to it. ("That's just Dad screaming again.") But when parents who seldom yell become genuinely angry and express it by their tone of voice, the children will pay attention and respond to it.

Parents who communicate effectively with their children:

• Allow their children to express their thoughts and feelings without fear. Being able to do this is why so many people visit therapists. If every parent were a good listener, therapists would be out of business.

• Let their children know they are interested in what they have to say.

• Help the child feel that he is accepted and respected as a person even though the parent might not agree with him.

- Use a friendly tone of voice even when what the child is saying is unacceptable.
- Pay full attention to the child when she is talking.
- Do not interrupt child when he is talking.
- Look directly at the child when she is talking and maintain good eye contact.
- Do not criticize the child's speech, grammar or content.

- Good communication helps us form good relationships, develop problem solving skills, and learn about the world.

- To communicate effectively with a child, it is important to give him the same respect and attention you would give to a close friend.

- Some roadblocks to good communication are:
  - monologues
  - ridiculing
  - criticizing
  - being condescending (talking in baby talk)

- The techniques of good communication include:
  - listening in an empathetic, non judgemental way
  - keeping your voice friendly and your mind open
  - allowing for disagreements

- Instead of asking a child what she did at school that day (and risking a one-word answer), prime the pump by talking about what you did that day.

- Communication is thought of as a "talking" skill, but the first step toward communication is being a good listener. There are two kinds of listening: Passive Listening, and Active Listening.

- To practise Passive Listening — Allow the child to talk freely. Don't interrupt except for encouraging nods of the head and the occasional "Uh huh's". If you feel the child does not feel understood, switch to Active Listening.

- Active Listening — Take what the child has said and paraphrase, saying it back to her in a different way. This gives her a chance to correct you or expand her thoughts.

- Asking Questions — Use the 5 W's: Who, What, Why, Where and When, to find out more about what your child is saying.

- When talking to children, there are essentially two kinds of questions: Open Questions and Closed Questions.

- Open Questions try to discover the child's viewpoint, and require more than a one-word answer. They make it easier for the child to communicate. Example: "How did losing the game today make you feel?"

- Closed Questions look for specific facts and tend to shut off communication. They can also be interpreted by the child as a means of parental control. Closed questions can be answered with one word. Example: "Did you win the game today?"

- There are two types of messages — "I" Messages and "You" Messages. An "I" message means that you are taking responsibility for a problem. Example: "I can't vacuum your room for you if it isn't cleaned up." A "You" message assigns blame. Example: "You didn't clean up your room."

- Anger is an essential human emotion because it lets us know when something is wrong. The key to anger is to express it properly. It is all a matter of degree. We let ourselves become angry in order to get immediate results. Instead, we should let our children know we are angry (and why) in a firm voice.

The family meeting

T he family meeting is a regularly scheduled discussion in which all members of the family are invited to talk about important family matters. In a family meeting, no person has a stronger voice or position than any other. In this way, the family may be viewed as a partnership in which all the members get together on a regular basis to solve problems, plan activities and improve relationships. Everyone is invited to present problems to the group and to offer solutions. Even very young children can participate.

This is a relatively new idea resulting from the movement in our society towards social equality and mutual respect. The idea of mutual respect is difficult for some adults to apply to children. That's because many of us find it hard to have respect for our children. We love them but how often do we respect a child's ideas or welcome his participation in family decisions? This is an important point, because our self esteem is greatly influenced by the amount of respect given to us. And it is an accepted fact that a child's self esteem is crucial to everything from his academic success to his mental health. We believe that respect and self esteem are as important to children as they are to adults, if not more. So why not begin to teach children that their ideas and help is wanted and even needed by the family from as early as three or four years old?

The idea of *participation* is another reason why the family meeting is so important. Children who participate in family meetings have a sense of being valued, productive members of the family. It provides a non-confrontational way of solving family disputes as well as running the family's day to day business. And, because everyone participates and agrees on the decisions, it's easier to establish cooperation regarding rules and regulations.

The family meeting is also a useful place to teach children how to have respect for others. We show mutual respect when we, as a group, take everyone's wishes and ideas into consideration. We show lack of respect when we demand that someone else (usually a child) do what we want. Asking a person for her ideas is an indication that her opinions are valued. Children are seldom asked for solutions to family problems. They are usually told what to do, and only rarely included in decision making.

Sharing decision-making power is not always an easy thing for a parent to do. Giving up our position as the only authority can be threatening. It goes totally against the way most of us have been raised. It may be difficult at first, but learning to share responsibility with your children will pay off in the long run. After all, being able to make wise decisions comes from being given responsibility, as well as the opportunity to test out ideas.

Shawn is thirteen and wants to baby sit his three siblings. He feels embarrassed when the family hires a sitter, and he knows of other thirteen year olds that get paid to baby sit. He already spontaneously handles some situations that arise, and feels he does it well. His parents, on the other hand, don't feel he is ready for the responsibility. They feel better when their 18 year old neighbour baby sits.

Shawn brings the question up at a meeting. "How much money do you pay the baby sitter?" he asks.

"Five dollars an hour," he is told.

"I'd be happy to do it for half that," Shawn says.

"It's not a question of money Shawn, we just don't think you're ready. Looking after three children is a huge responsibility."

"But some of my friends are already doing it. What makes it all right for them and not for me?"

"Why don't you let him do it," asks his younger brother George. "We'll promise to behave especially well for Shawn."

"Well," his mother says thoughtfully, "we are going next door for a party on Friday night. Maybe we could try it then."

All the boys — not just Shawn — were very happy about this. That Friday night they had a good time playing together, and actually went to bed on time, something that they had always resisted in the past.

A few days later, George asked if he could stay up late one night to watch a special program.

"I don't know George, it's past your bedtime," said his parents.

Normally George would have sulked at this, but instead he said, "I think I'm old enough to stay up later. I'll bring it up at the family meeting."

The children now see the family meeting as a place where changes can happen. The meeting helped them find a solution to one problem, as well as diffuse another.

These meetings are important character builders. It gives children an opportunity to try out ideas, to see their ideas followed through, and is an excellent way for them to learn about choices and consequences. These are all vital if children are going to learn about responsibility. And remember, everyone has veto power over decisions. That means you as parents never have to go along with any decision that you simply can't live with.

Todd and Emanuel are 11 and 12 years old, and have been invited to go for an overnight camping trip down by the river. They think they should be allowed to go, because their friend's older brothers are going to be with them.

"The rule in our family has always been that we can go for sleep-overs as long as there is an adult there," the children say. "And Tommy's brother is 18 years old so we think we should be able to go."

Dad listens and thinks about what they have said. "I'm very uncomfortable with the idea of you guys sleeping out somewhere with someone I don't know. The family rule has always been that you could have sleep-overs at homes where we know the people. I'm not sure this situation fits the rule."

"But Dad, that's not fair. We'll be with an adult."

"No. I just don't think this is safe enough. The old rule has to stand. We can see about changing it as you get older."

The rule for family meetings is: if even one person can't go along with a decision, whatever was in place before remains the order of the day. Although the children did not get their way, the fact that they had previously agreed to this rule makes it easier to accept the "no". Plus, Todd and Emmanuel have the option of changing the circumstances in the future. In fact, Dad could have used the meeting to encourage them to look for alternatives. At the next meeting he can suggest they go camping with a friend's dad, or invite him to come along. Knowing it is possible to change the rule also makes it easier for children to accept being told "no".

The family meeting —
democratically speaking

It is recommended that meetings be held at least once a week, at a determined time, in order to ensure that any problems will be addressed as they arise. It will be helpful if you take the time to make these meetings special. That means not holding them during meal times, always starting on time, and not cancelling them unless there is a good reason. You should make every effort to follow through on any agreements or decisions that are made at the meetings. If no agreement is reached, the matter can be tabled until the next meeting. Tabling means that the topic under discussion is unresolved and will be talked about again at the next meeting:

> *"This problem is going to take some thinking about. Let's all try and come up with solutions during the week, and we can take another look at it during next week's meeting."*

It's also a good idea to brainstorm *(See Problem Solving, Chapter 10)* as many solutions as possible, then ask which might work best and which to try. This teaches children how to be critical, discriminating and creative.

As we have stated before, the basis of the family meeting is equality: everyone has the right to a say in the rules and decisions of the family. Even when he is too young to participate in a family meeting (younger than three and a half years old), children should still be present in order to absorb the tone and idea of the meeting and then be ready to join in when they are old enough. No one may force his view on the rest of the family. However, people can be persuasive, and are encouraged to air their views fully. All decisions are arrived at democratically (by consensus). Although this might sound difficult to pull off, it's often an easier approach than the old method where the parents were "super human" and bore the burden of every decision. But you must also remember that your opinions as parents' count too. Some parents' go the opposite way and give up all influence. The democratic approach is neither a giving up of all authority, nor the wielding of total authority, but the sharing of decision making power.

Consensus

In a family meeting, it is important that no one walks away feeling that his needs were not taken into consideration, or that he was railroaded into something. For this reason, majority rule is not used. Instead, decisions are not made unless everyone agrees to abide by the decision. In other words, no decision is taken unless there is unanimous consent. If everyone can't agree, the topic is put aside until the next meeting.

> *Twelve year old Alison doesn't want to go to school. She says that virtually all of the girls in her grade belong to cliques, making it impossible for her to form friendships. This uncomfortable social scene has been made worse by the fact that she doesn't get along with her teacher. At the family meeting, Alison tells her parents about her problems, and demands that the family set up a home schooling program.*
>
> *Neither of Alison's parents thinks this is a good idea. Her father works full time, and her mother has a part time job. Not only do they not have enough time to teach Alison at home, they believe Alison should overcome her social problems at school. They know that she has always been a shy child, and was upset when she recently had to move away from her best (and only) friend.*
>
> *By talking to her about her shyness, her parents feel that they at least have the problem out in the open, and have found out why she has been so moody and quiet since they moved to the new house. They now talk with her about ways to solve the problem.*
>
> *"I'm glad you brought this up, Alison. We've noticed you've been unhappy but we didn't know why. Let's see*

what we can do about helping you. Is there anyone at school you would like to be friends with?"

"Well yes, there is a girl called Melody who is very nice when she isn't with the other girls."

"OK. Maybe you could invite her for lunch on the weekend. That way you two could get to know each other better away from the other kids."

"I would like to do that, but I don't know if she would want to. And I still don't want to go to that school any more. For one thing, I think I could concentrate better on my school work at home," she says, not giving up.

Her parents feel for Alison, but they can't go along with her home schooling plan.

"For one thing," her mom explains, "I have my hands full working part time. I don't have time to learn your curriculum. But I'll tell you what — why don't we all get together and talk to your teacher?"

But Alison is too disappointed to entertain any options. "I hate that school. I just don't want to go to it any more."

Mom gives her a hug and says, "I know you aren't happy there right now, and you're disappointed we won't go along with keeping you home from school. But I'm really glad you know you can talk to us about this. It's hard to break into a new school. It's going to take time. Let's think about how we can help you make it easier. We can talk about it this week."

Alison is not happy, but feels good about getting it off her chest and says, "OK".

Even though the problem wasn't "solved", the family is on its way to helping Alison. And she no longer feels she is in it alone. Sometimes there is no perfect solution to a problem, but the family meeting did help Alison and her parents come closer together rather than be pushed apart.

When a decision is made, it is maintained until the next meeting. This underscores the feeling that the family meeting is a serious family institution. People also learn that inappropriate decisions present difficulties that are hard to live with during the week. By the next meeting, everyone is ready to make a more appropriate decision.

The Federovs and their six children are trying to decide what to do about the children's bicycles at night. The problem is trying to fit the bikes and the cars in the garage at the same time. At a family meeting, everyone takes a crack at solving it.

"Why not just leave them at the side of the house?" says Tanya.

""No. They'll get stolen there," counters Peter. "They have to go in the garage."

"I like to put the car in the garage after dinner so I don't forget," says dad. "So maybe you should put them in then."

"No," Natasha wails. "We all like to ride our bikes after dinner. We'll put them in just before it's time to come in for the night."

Mom and Dad aren't crazy about this solution, but because they can't come up with a better one, they decide to go along with it. But on the next school day when Mom goes to get in the car, there is a barricade of bikes piled up behind it. She has to spend valuable time finding one of the kids to move the bikes. Mornings are the busiest, most hectic times at the Federov house. Mom is late for work one morning and two of the children are late for school. At the next meeting, Mom points out that the bicycle rule is not working out. So other solutions are brainstormed. Finally, Tanya comes up with one.

"There doesn't seem to be room in the garage for the car and the bikes," she says, "so lets put the bikes in the shed in the garden."

No one can come up with a better solution, so a vote is taken and it passes.

Getting consensus is important in a democratic system. If you are having trouble getting consensus, sometimes simply recognizing a person's objection will be enough.

The Weinbergs are having a problem with arguing. Jasmine, fifteen, doesn't like the bickering that is constantly going on between her younger sister Ruth, and their mother. She brings it up at a family meeting.

"You two fight all the time," Jasmine says. "The worst is when I have friends over. People are starting to comment on it. Your fighting is getting so embarrassing, I'm not even comfortable having company in."

"I agree that Ruth and I are arguing a lot lately. But it's usually because Ruth feels left out and seems to want me to do something about it. But I feel that it's fair that you should be able to spend time with your friends alone."

"You see. You're always taking Jasmine's side," Ruth points out.

At this point, Dad jumps in. "OK. I can see there's a problem here. First of all, Ruth feels left out when Jasmine's friends are over. Is that right?"

Ruth nods.

Dad continues. "Mom obviously feels caught in the middle, especially when Ruth demands that she do something about it."

Mom nods.

Ruth says tearfully: "Mom and Jasmine are both against me. Sometimes I feel all alone in this house."

Dad says: "So Ruth feels that whenever Jasmine's friends come over, she should be able to play with them. And she feels we should back her up. So the question is, how should we handle this?"

"I feel that when my friends come over, I should be able to play with them alone," Jasmine offers. "It's not that I don't like you Ruth — I do, and I play with you a lot. It's not that I don't want to be with you. But sometimes my friends and I want to talk privately."

"Yeah. You want to talk about boys."

Jasmine blushes. "Well, maybe."

"But I'll be on my own too much. I like playing with you and your friends."

"Actually, I can see two very valid points of view here," says Mom. "On the one hand, sometimes we want to have some privacy with our friends, but on the other, nobody likes to be told she is not wanted. It hurts her feelings. I have an idea. Would you like to hear it? Ruth will give Jasmine and her friends some time together

when they want it, and Jasmine will include Ruth when they are doing something they know she would like to do."

"But what will I do when her friends are over?" Ruth asks.

"Why don't you invite your own friends over," Jasmine says, "or play with your computer?"

"Would you be willing to give that a try for a week?" asks Mom. "We can see how it's going at the next meeting."

Ruth thinks about it for a minute and then agrees to try it.

"I think you're on the right track here," says Dad. "And this will stop Mom from having to be in the middle."

"Yes. I hate the idea that anyone would feel I was taking sides. I'm really glad you told me you feel that way Ruth."

The solution the Weinbergs came up with was not necessarily the right one for every family. The point is, they were able to reach consensus on a possible solution. If it doesn't work out, they have a chance to try again at the next meeting. Also, by listening to each other talk about their feelings, they came to a greater understanding of what the problems were. Not only did this help patch up the relationship between the sisters, but that of Ruth and her mother. These meetings also help clear up misinterpretations. For instance, Ruth thought that Jasmine was rejecting her because she didn't like her, which was not true. Ruth also mistakenly believed she had the right to do exactly what she wanted. The meeting also let Mom know she was being perceived as taking sides, something she didn't want to do. She was then able to convince Ruth that she wasn't.

Of course, all decisions cannot be made at a family meeting. Some decisions, like financial matters, are inappropriate for children to be involved in. However, when possible, children can be asked to express their feelings and concerns about related decisions, for example, moving or buying a new car. This helps them to feel they really matter.

Tom Watts is a single father with a 16 year old son, Brenden. The two have a good relationship, but Brenden was devastated when his mother left the family and moved to another country with her boyfriend. Even though he is close to his father, his mother's departure has left Brenden feeling confused and insecure. Now he learns that his father has just been offered a great new job in another city. Brenden doesn't want to leave his friends and the garage band he's in. Father and son talk about it at an impromptu family meeting.

"Dad," Brenden asks, "What's the matter with the job you've got now? I thought you liked it here."

"I do like it here, but this new job offer is something I've worked hard for all of my professional life. Not only that, but we'll have a lot more money to spend."

"Why do we need more money? We're doing OK now. I've got some really close friends here, and the band is starting to take off a little. I think we should stay."

"You're right, we are doing OK for money now. But I would like to retire some day. And besides, you will be

going to University soon and that costs a lot of money. I'm trying to think past today and plan for tomorrow."

The reality of what his dad is saying sinks in. Brenden realizes he won't be able to fight the move to another city. A look of profound sadness comes over his face. "I guess you're right Dad," he says, close to tears. "But I'll never find a friend as good as Chris, and I've put so much time and effort into the band."

"It sounds like it's going to be hard to leave your friends. I know you and Chris are close and that the band means a lot to you. Starting over again — trying to find new friends who share your interests is not easy. You don't find a friend like Chris overnight. It takes a lot of courage to make this move. But at the very least, this will give us a chance to spend time together, meet new people and start a new life. What would you think of inviting Chris out to spend summer vacation at our new home?"

"Yeah. I'd like that. It would be fun showing him around the city."

Tom took his son's concerns seriously. Even though he had made his decision, he tried to understand what Brenden was going through. Rather than getting angry when Brenden balked, he tried to explain why he made the decision: why it was important for both of them that he take this new job. Once Brenden realized that his father understood what he was feeling, he was able to concede that his father might be right. Tom was also able to come up with a few good ideas that would help Brenden accept the move, especially the one regarding inviting Chris for the summer. He recognized the importance of the friendship, and was able to think of a way to soften the blow.

Roadblocks to a successful family meeting

Obviously, a Family Meeting is different from a casual conversation around the dinner table. The meeting is more structured and its decisions carry more weight. Learning how to do it right can be difficult for some families. Families with older children who have been used to an autocratic style may see the meeting as just another way of controlling behaviour and coming up with new rules. They may not believe that their opinions carry any weight or that they can really change the results.

In addition, if children are not used to having to come up with ideas and solutions on their own, it may take them some time to learn the ropes.

One way to get around this problem is to learn to use the appropriate language during meetings. Your primary purpose should be to include the children in the meeting while opening them up to participation. To do this, use open ended questions ("what do you think would work best for this problem?"), allow for pauses so the children can add comments, and avoid searching for blame. Don't be in a hurry to rush in with solutions for them, let them come up with some suggestions first. Remind yourself that it will take you a little time to learn how to act during a meeting. Don't get discouraged if it doesn't get off to a great start. Learning the democratic process takes time, but it will work in the long run.

Keep in mind that, particularly in the beginning, it is not as important to come up with the best solutions to problems as it is for your children to take part in the process of a meeting, to experience first hand the democratic process and what it can mean to interpersonal relationships. We have seen young children bursting with pride after having helped solve a problem as mundane as deciding to use place mats on the table to help control the mess. The point is, you are including them in the way the family is run. And you will be surprised even very young children can participate in meetings.

> *The Cardinals have a four year old boy, Jimmy. At their first family meeting, the problem of puddles of water caused by melting snow from boots is brought up.*
>
> *Jimmy says: "The water's there 'cause it's snowing outside."*
>
> *Dad says: "You're right. The snow from outside is coming inside — on our boots. I wonder if we could figure out a way of keeping the entrance hall drier?"*
>
> *"Why don't we bang our feet outside the front door and shake the snow off?" offers Jimmy."*

Although this was a very simple and only partial solution to the problem, Jimmy's idea shows how good even young children can be at problem solving if they are given a chance. Think of all the simple solutions to the tiny problems that bother us every day, that young children could find. The point is, once they have had even one solution accepted by the family at a meeting, they will feel valued for their suggestions and more inclined to follow the rules that the rest of the family comes up with. At the very least, this is better than bugging Jimmy to stop spreading snow around every time he walks in the door. The important thing is that Jimmy's parents didn't try for the "perfect solution". You will find that very often the process itself is more important than the decision.

Introducing the first meeting

Once the parents have decided that family meetings are important, their next step is to invite the children. This preparing of the ground is important if your family is going to approach the meetings with an open mind. If you do it skillfully, you will allay the fears of your children (things like: "I'm just going to be bossed around," or, "I'm being railroaded into this). Be enthusiastic and positive. Start off by saying something like this:

"Dad and I have learned about an exciting idea called Family Meetings. We think it would be a great way for our family to plan fun things to do, share jobs more fairly, help each other with problems and just generally come up with ideas that would make our family better. We know you kids have really creative minds and we'd like you to help us keep things running smoothly."

Having your children come to the first meeting of their own free will is important. Talk about specifics: "The meetings would be held once a week; someone different will chair each meeting," etc. If there is any resistance, the following remarks should help:

- "Do you have any questions about the weekly family meeting we would like to hold?"
- "Who would like to do it?"
- "Is there anyone who doesn't want to do it?" "Why don't you want to do it?"
- "It's up to you, but if you don't feel like coming, we would miss having your ideas to help the family."
- "The decisions made by the people attending the meeting will have to be carried out whether a particular family member is there or not. Does that sound fair?"

If none of the children accepts the invitation to join the first meeting, the parents should start anyway. The children might end up joining in even though they may appear to be stand-offish. With the children who have decided to join, agree on the place and time of the meeting. This agreement forms the starting point of the democratic family meeting.

The first meeting

The parents take on the official duties only for the first few meetings, until the children are ready to take their turn (the chair should be at least five or six years old). One parent could be the chairperson and the other the recording secretary. A good idea is to have the least dominant parent become the first chairperson, demonstrating early how new patterns of interaction can work.

At the first meeting, discuss what the chairperson does. The duties may include starting the meeting on time, deciding who has the floor, and not allowing interruptions. The chair speaks last.

The recording secretary keeps the minutes of each meeting, reads the minutes of previous meetings and posts the agenda. Children learning how to write will enjoy this job.

Determine the rotation of roles. Will they change each week or month?

Make sure the first few meetings are positive and fun so that the children will feel good about them. Planning a fun outing might be a good way to start.

Marjorie and John have three children: Nine year old Peter, seven year old Anne, and three year old Carl. They both feel that their family functions fairly well, but they do have a few problem areas: bedtime, homework and fighting between the children. They took a parenting course, mainly to improve the communication with their children as well as to solve the few problems they had.

They led up to the first meeting by Mom saying: "Children, at our parenting course it was suggested that a wonderful way for families to help each other have a happier and closer family, would be to hold meetings every week. I thought it sounded like a good idea, and so did your dad, but we wanted to see what you thought. We would have a meeting each week where we would talk about things we could do together, as well as how we could become a closer and happier family. Would you like to do that?"

Peter goes along with it, and Carl agrees with his big brother. But Anne hesitates. "Gee, I don't know. I've never heard of this before. Do we have to do it every week? What if it gets boring? Do I still have to come?"

"Those are good questions Anne," Dad says. "We would like everyone to come, because we will be making decisions that affect us all. I'll tell you what though, if there are things about the meeting that you don't like, we can change it so it's more fun for you. But if you really don't want to come, you don't have to, although we would miss having your ideas to help the family. Why don't you try coming to at least the first one?"

Once they agree to come, it is important for children to realize that their solutions are taken seriously, even if you can see that there is a better solution. Sometimes it is better to accept their imperfect solution, (at least until the next meeting), in order to help them improve their judgement, and to avoid bickering at the meetings. This is especially important with children that are into power, and who are liable to dig in their heels and be stubborn if thwarted too many times at meetings.

Ten year old Andrew's mother spends a lot of time every evening trying to get him to do his homework. Andrew doesn't like being told what to do. His mother feels that she knows what is right for him and finds it frustrating that he won't listen to her. The problem of homework is brought up at a family meeting.

"It seems that we are arguing a lot about your homework," Mom says. "I thought we might try scheduling a time for you to do it every night. That way I wouldn't have to constantly be at you about it."

Andrew jumps at the idea. "OK. Great. I'll do it every night just before I go to bed."

"Oh no," says his mother. "If you wait until then you'll be too tired to concentrate. I think as soon as you get home from school is a much better time."

"But that's when I usually throw the ball around with Cliff," Andrew says, beginning to get agitated. "Before I go to bed is the only time there is nothing else to do."

"But if you get it over with right away you can have the whole evening free. Otherwise, it will be hanging over our heads all night."

"No it won't," says Andrew, bouncing up and down in his seat. "That's when I want to do it!"

At this point, Mother perceives that the discussion is about to degenerate into a power struggle. She decides to back off for the time being.

"All right Andrew. If you go to bed at nine, what time should you start your homework?"

"It takes me an hour, so I should start it at eight," Andrew responds.

"Good. Then we'll try that for the coming week. We can see how it has been going at the next meeting."

Mom wisely let Andrew try it his way, even though she was sure it was not the best solution. She did it to avoid having a pitched battle during the meeting, and also because she knew that the only way Andrew was going to learn a better approach was to experience what it would be like doing it his way. As it turned out, Andrew had real trouble finishing his homework that week, and on one occasion was even reprimanded by his teacher. At the next meeting, he still wanted to stick with the late schedule. But after three weeks of this, he himself offered to do the homework right after dinner. One reason for this is that his mom is now much more relaxed about his homework. She got off his back and left it up to him. He is now free to solve the problem, instead of fighting with Mom about it.

Family meetings — practically speaking

The main function of a family meeting is to develop good, cooperative family relationships. These positive relationships develop because each family member:

- shares in the decision making power
- is treated with respect and dignity
- has a right to choice
- is a partner in the family (at least in accordance to his ability and responsibilities)
- helps to establish rules

What does the family meeting provide? The family meeting provides an opportunity for:

- sharing ideas
- being listened to
- giving encouragement to each other

- sharing responsibilities
- bringing up concerns
- resolving conflicts and complaints
- planning family fun and routines
- sharing positive and negative feelings

Guidelines for a family meeting

1. Schedule your meetings weekly, or even more frequently with younger children, who can only concentrate for short periods of time.

Reasons to meet weekly
- provides an opportunity to follow up on suggestions to see how previously made agreements and decisions are going
- provides an opportunity to deal with problems as they arise
- demonstrates consistency
- allows for problems to be given full attention at an agreed upon time

2. Alternate the chairperson

(The chair's job is to recognize whose turn it is to speak, and generally keep order.) Having a different member of the family chair the meeting (from age 6 on):
- provides opportunities for leadership
- shows your children you have confidence in them
- teaches democratic procedures

3. Keep minutes

(The secretary's job is to record all decisions and topics.) Having a record of what was decided at each conference:

- underlines the importance of family decisions
- indicates the solutions to problems, which is encouraging
- helps people remember the rules
- helps people remember their responsibilities

4. Plan out the meeting (See Agenda):

Some families don't like to have the meeting structured too much. Even though we recommend a structure, you should do whatever works best for your family. In any event, you will need a time keeper to make sure the meeting begins at the time agreed upon and, once started, doesn't drag on too long.

The time keeper's job, the person who keeps track of how much time is allotted to each item on the agenda, is important because it:
- helps keep the meeting structured
- helps people learn how to schedule their time
- helps stay focused on the issues
- helps people be concise

5. Get everyone to participate:

You can encourage everyone to participate by:
- allowing children to give opinions first so they don't feel intimidated or dominated
- pick a time when everyone is available
- present it in a positive, enthusiastic way

6. Limit the complaints:

Don't let your family meeting degenerate into negative gripe sessions. In order to ensure that your family enjoys

these regular meetings:
- always be moving towards solutions;
- don't let gripes continue;
- make sure everyone realizes there are always solutions to problems;
- remind everyone that seeking a solution is the real goal of the meeting;
- point out how well you feel the meetings are going.

7. Establish household chores by:

- making a list of all the chores in the home as well as who has volunteered to do them;
- discussing when, where and how the chores are to be done;
- scheduling a time to teach children how to do chores they have never done.

8. Make sure agreements are kept:

- All agreements made are to be kept until the next meeting.
- When agreements are not kept, logical consequences are used. For example, if someone agrees to make the plans involved in going to the movies but doesn't follow up, the trip to the movies is cancelled.

9. Treat everyone's concerns as equally important:

- Make sure everyone realizes that all family members' issues are important.
- Give everyone the right to bring up his own problems. In fact, encourage children to bring up their problems and ideas.

- Make sure the problems of the parents are not given precedence, or the children will see it as *your* meeting and lose interest.

10. Plan family fun

It's important for families to have recreation, to spend time together and enjoy each other. Using the family meeting to plan family fun:
- brings excitement to the meeting
- makes everyone feel positive about the meeting and produces a happy atmosphere in the family
- gives children a feeling of belonging

Dealing with non participation

In some families, one parent will not want to participate in the meeting at all. The reasons could be:
- he has little confidence in his children's abilities to understand family matters
- he prefers to make all decisions

Having family meetings can be a very big step, and it's not hard to understand how some parents would find it hard to do. This is a common problem, but you can go ahead and have the meeting anyway. Your spouse may decide to join later, but it is not a good idea to pressure him or her into it.

Fran Galloway takes care of most of the day to day matters concerning the children. Her husband, Bob, feels he is the breadwinner and therefore, head of the family, but acknowledges his wife's right to run the household the way she sees fit. Fran hears about the idea of family meetings from some other moms on the playground and thinks it might work very well for her three children. That night, she and Bob talk about it.

"Look," Bob tells her. "I make the money and you raise the kids. I feel very comfortable with that. But I don't see any reason to include the kids in the decision making of the house. I know they fight a lot, but I think that's because you are too lenient with them. They sure do what I tell them to do, especially when I raise my voice. Have meetings if you want, but I think you're wasting your time. And you can count me out. When I come home, I just want to relax."

"I think it would work a lot better if we all participated," Fran tells him. "But if you really don't want to, we'll do it without you."

After a couple of months, the behaviour of the children is greatly improved. So much so that even Bob notices the change in the quality of family life. One night out of curiosity, he asks if he can sit in on a meeting — just as an observer. Unable to sit quietly, Bob jumps in and offers his opinion on a number of topics. Although he doesn't vote on anything at this meeting, he tells Fran when it's over: "You know. I kind of enjoyed this. Maybe I'll come to the next meeting. Actually, I think this kind of thing might help my business if we did it at work."

If Bob had been pressured at the beginning, he would have either rebelled and become a staunch opponent of the meetings, or attended a few and been negative and uncooperative. But most open minded parents, if they see that family meetings work, will be overcome by curiosity (as Bob was) and at the very least feel much more open to the idea of family meetings. Also, a lot of people (Bob is one) don't like to do things that aren't their idea. By not pressuring him, he was able to make the choice to come to the meeting making it, in a way, his idea. The same principle applies to children who are unresponsive.

Why Some Parents Don't Want To Have A Meeting

> Don't have time: it's easier to
> make snap decisions yourself.

The reality is, if children are rebellious about their parents' decisions, the parents will have to spend more time (perhaps ten times as much), in dealing with the rebellion through threats and punishments, foot dragging and disobedience. In the long run, it takes less time to deal with meetings than it does to deal with uncooperative behaviour.

> Parents don't want to share the
> power they have always had.

You really don't lose power, you are sharing it with the children through consensus. Because everyone has veto power on decisions, you will never get steamrolled into doing something you don't agree with.

> Parents feel that their children are
> too self centred to make group decisions.

Some children are like that, but the family meeting is actually the solution to this problem. Giving children a chance to hear the viewpoints of others, and to experience cooperation, is an excellent way to instill social interest.

> Parents feel their values will be overturned (that the
> children will decide not to go to church, for example).

Forcing values on children doesn't teach values, in fact it often backfires into rebellion. Having good communication between you and your children is the best guarantee that you will be able to pass on your values.

Parents fear loss of respect for their authority.

On the contrary, your children's respect for you will increase. That's because meetings are a way of showing respect for them. And don't forget that your children model after you. Usually, parents who complain that their children don't respect them are the ones who don't demonstrate respect for their children.

The family meeting agenda

Every family can and will have different agendas. The following is a comprehensive list of agenda items that would cover most family business:

1. Things that are going well or
   have improved (encouragement).
2. Planning
3. Responsibilities
4. Improvements needed in family
5. Personal concerns

1. Things That Are Going Well

This is a good way to start off the meeting on the right foot (note: families that are having serious problems should *only* talk about the following positive things for the first few meetings in order to raise family morale.) Here are some examples:

- discuss good things about each family member
- discuss who has been helpful
- talk about warm feelings toward each other
- point out each other's strengths

- stress the healthy part of the family atmosphere
- discuss positive values in the family
- share positive things about one's life
- talk about what is improving in the family

   The above points will help create a feeling of belonging to the family; that the family is a good place to be.

2. Family Planning:

   This includes all of the day-to-day plans a family has to make, such as:
- menu planning
- transportation (to school, soccer practise etc.)
- weekly calendar (Thursday night: parents going to parenting class, baby sitter arriving at 7:00 etc.)
- special events, like birthdays, trips and movies;
- TV schedule (how often and what programs?)
- homework schedule
- morning and bedtime routines
- outside activities (brownies, karate, scouts, swimming etc.)
- family visits
- weekend routine
- allowances, spending, budgeting, purchasing gifts

3. Responsibilities:
- determining who will do what jobs
- who will teach children to do the jobs
- when will the jobs be done
- what is expected from the jobs
- how to rotate jobs
- how to remind people about the jobs

Sometimes with younger children, you have to break the task down into very specific jobs, for instance:

Shopping can be broken down into:
- making a shopping list
- shopping at food market
- putting away groceries

Cleaning bathrooms could involve:
- hanging up towels
- cleaning the toilets, sink and tub
- washing the mirror
- sweeping the bathroom floor, etc.

Other common jobs could include:
- cleaning own room
- picking up toys
- vacuuming
- dusting furniture
- cooking
- washing pots
- drying dishes and putting them away
- sweeping and washing kitchen floor
- making beds
- putting away clean clothes
- setting table
- washing dishes
- clearing table
- putting laundry in laundry basket
- cleaning sink

4. Problem Solving:
(See Problem Solving, Chapter 10)
- discussion about rules
- what to do when rules are broken
- problems about fighting, sharing, jobs, etc.
- problems about emotional outbursts, temper, unfairness and how to achieve justice in the family
- brainstorming solutions.

5. Personal Problems:
• sharing problems with family members.

This can include worries about money and personal relationships. For example, a child might tell the family that his best friend won't talk to him. The point is, if any or all members of the family are having problems, the family meeting should be thought of as a good place to look for help in solving them, as well as a source of comfort and support.

Good Reasons For Holding Family Meetings:
• it elicits cooperation;
• empowers children by giving them a say in decision making;
• children don't feel dominated;
• children are respected;
• it teaches responsibility;
• it helps children learn problem solving;
• it gives the family a sense of closeness through sharing;
• it provides a forum for encouraging statements;
• it provides intimacy;
• it takes some of the burden of making decisions off of the parents;
• it helps overcome sibling rivalry;
• it raises self esteem.

Ground rules for conducting a family meeting
1. Only one person at a time can speak
2. No put downs allowed
3. Stay on topic
4. Obey the chairperson
5. Be open to adding ground rules

Family meeting do's and don'ts

- *Do select a certain date of each week for the family meeting.*
- *Do invite all members of the family to participate.*
- *Do encourage everyone to contribute and express ideas.*
- *Do rotate the chairpersonship.*
- *Do maintain parliamentary order, providing each member with the opportunity to express him or herself freely.*
- *Do feel obliged to listen to others.*
- *Do not use the meeting as a gripe session, but as a source of problem solving.*
- *Do expect each person to present a solution when expressing a complaint.*
- *Do emphasize what can be done (the dishes have to be done), rather than what members must do (you do the dishes).*
- *Do let children experience the consequences of a "wrong" decision (if it's not immoral or unsafe).*
- *Do wait until the next session to alter a decision.*
- *Do accept the family meeting as the family's decision making body.* ·
- *Do understand that it is not one person shouldering the full responsibility for the household's healthy functioning.*
- *Do commit to the idea that it is truly important that children accept responsibility, even more important than the concept that things must run smoothly all the time.*
- *Don't call a meeting every time someone wants one. Most things are not so urgent they have to be settled on the spot. Emergency meetings should be kept for emergencies.*
- *Don't force members to attend — participation is not obligatory.*

- The Family Meeting is a new idea based on the movement of society towards social equality and mutual respect.

- The Family Meeting teaches children the valuable life skills of problem solving, social interest and working with others.

- Families that hold regular family meetings are more cooperative and less competitive. This is because there is no authority figure to make the decisions for everyone.

- Some parents are hesitant to give up their authority to the Family Meeting. But in reality, the meetings make life easier for them because problems are solved in a non-confrontational manner.

- All decisions are made by consensus. That means everyone has a veto.

- When a decision is made, it is maintained until the next meeting, when it can be discussed again.

- Even when no decision is reached regarding a particular problem, the family benefits from being able to air its thoughts and feelings.

- Even very young children can feel like a valuable member of the family by helping to solve simple problems.

Sibling rivalry and fighting

"The dangers of favouritism can hardly be overdramatized. Almost every discouragement in childhood springs from the feeling that someone else is preferred."

—Alfred Adler

The dynamics of fighting

When children fight, it's important to understand the family dynamics that are at the root of it. For instance, have you ever noticed that when one child is misbehaving, the other child becomes good? That's because when there is a fight, often one of the children will take on the role of the "good child" and use this to gain approval from the parents. But this "good child" may only be trying to appear better than a sibling. So, by responding to the uncooperative behaviour of one child, we are essentially intensifying the competition between both children.

One interesting theory that explains the underlying reason siblings take on these "good" child "bad" child roles is that they want to move into the position of being the favourite of the parents. Often one parent will have a favourite sibling. This favouritism has nothing to do with loving one child more than an another, but in finding one child easier to get along with, easier to get close to and better behaved. This child perceives (often unconsciously and sometimes erroneously), that she is the favourite, and will try to keep that position. The fact is, children don't want to be loved equally, they want to be loved *more*, or better still, exclusively. The child who perceives that he is not in the favoured position may feel jealous and angry towards his sibling; "If it weren't for you, I would be the favourite." He will therefore try to get back at the favourite child and even wish him out of the family. At the same time, however, he can also deeply love his siblings and enjoy their company. These conflicting emotions actually exist simultaneously. The upshot of this is something any parent knows, siblings fight.

In order to stay in the favoured position, the child has to constantly point out to the parent that the sibling is causing difficulties. The unfavoured child fights back to get even for making him look bad.

One way to help the child who feels she is in the unfavoured position is to spend time with her and talk about her feelings. If she tells you she feels unfavoured, acknowledge her feelings, and discuss ways to solve the problem. Reassure her that you do in fact love both children equally. Listening to her, telling her that you love her, and spending quality time with them is the best way to prevent sibling rivalry because it enhances your relationship with her. Unfortunately sibling rivalry never goes away completely, but if a child tells you that she thinks you love a sibling more than her or complains of unfairness, treat it as a great opportunity to work on the problem.

> *Heather, who is 10, is watching her favourite TV program when her 12 year old brother Mark comes in and changes the channel. Heather yells at the top of her lungs: "I was watching that show! Put it back on right now or I'm going to tell Mom."*

> *Mark says: "You've been watching your shows all day. Now it's my turn."*

> *Heather continues to scream at him: "Put that show back on!"*

> *Mark balls his fist at her: "If you don't shut up, you're going to get creamed."*

> *Heather moves towards the TV to change it and Mark pushes her away. She falls and acts as if she is hurt and runs off to her mother. She now has two outrages to report: he took over the TV, and physically hurt her.*

> *Mom goes into the TV room and confronts Mark: "I have told you and told you not to hit your sister. She's younger and smaller than you. You should be ashamed of yourself. How could you be such a bully?"*

> *Now Mom feels he should be punished. "Go to your room and stay there until dinner time. Here Heather, you can finish watching your show."*

> *Mark storms out of the room, saying over his shoulder: "You always take her side. She doesn't own the TV you know. I hate Heather and I hate you too!"*

Heather ignores this and says, "You're right Mom, Mark really is a bully."

Mom's observation about Mark was correct; he did hurt Heather and used his power to get what he wanted. What she didn't get was Mark's underlying motivation. Ever since the birth of his younger sister, he has constantly gotten into trouble because of her. He feels deep resentment because he perceives himself to be the unfavoured child, and Heather as Mom's favourite. Even though he frequently tells his parents how he feels, he is ignored. "Oh, don't be ridiculous Mark," is the usual retort.

Mark doesn't feel he is understood, or taken seriously. He is deeply discouraged. Although he does well at school and has a lot of friends, he doesn't feel he belongs when he is at home. His parents can't understand how he can be so successful outside the family, yet cause so much friction when he is home. They have missed how devastating it is for Mark to perceive himself as the disfavoured child.

In order to help Mark, Mom needs to recognize that the problem goes much deeper than who watches what TV program. She should spend some time working on the bigger issues involved in the family dynamic. Essentially, there is a short term and a long term problem here. The short term problem is the TV schedule. At the moment of the sibling fight over the TV, Mom should have turned the TV off and told the children: "Since you can't agree on what to watch, the TV will have to stay off until you learn how to get along."

She can also decrease the competition by not showing any favouritism. One of the best ways to do this is to not take sides. When children are together in a room and one starts misbehaving, the parents should treat the situation as a group disturbance rather than as one individual being wrong. Request that both children leave the room together and may return only when the problem is worked out. This teaches them to respect the rights of other people in the family.

If, when using this strategy, the "good child" feels it is unfair, you must realize that both children play a part in any disturbance even though one may look more guilty. The only exception to the non-involvement rule is if you think there will be serious physical harm done, in which case you have to separate them. Remember, your overall goal is to decrease competition, while having all the children come out on top.

Another important point is that the incident with the TV has less to do with right and wrong, but much more to do with competition between the siblings over the love of the parents. It's Mom's job to teach them the skills of how to get along, but it is their responsibility to actually do it. Therefore, she can bring up the problem of the TV schedule at the family meeting, and be involved in finding a fair solution.

The long term problem is the feeling of favouritism and resulting competition between the siblings. Mom has to help Mark realize that he is loved. She can prove this by spending one-on-one time with him and taking his concerns seriously. Talking to him and practicing Active Listening (*See Communication, Chapter 7*) will help Mark get his feelings about not being loved enough out in the open.

Talking about sibling rivalry

The best way to deal with sibling rivalry is to get it out in the open. Keep in mind however, that this needs to be handled with great sensitivity and tact. You need not raise the issue of favouritism yourself. But be on the lookout for evidence that one of your children may feel you are being partial to a sibling. You accomplish this by bringing up the subject of fighting with your children in a calm, neutral situation such as a family meeting. Here is a sample dialogue involving six year old Samantha and eight year old Max.

> *Mom says: "It looks like the anger and fighting between you two has really increased this summer. Would you agree?"*

(Note: Don't assume that the children will automatically agree with you. Always take time to see what they are thinking. Sometimes your assumptions will be correct, but you haven't stated them exactly right. Asking gives your children a chance to correct you or restate the problem from their point of view.)

> *Samantha quickly points out: "That's because Max is always taking my things and hitting me."*

> *"That's not true," counters Max. "You let me play with your stuff one day and then change your mind the next."*

> *"I only did that once. You're lying."*

> *"You see," Mom says. "This is exactly what I'm talking about. You two are just not getting along."*

> *Mom now asks an open ended question in order to start the process of getting to the root of the problem.*

> *"Now let me ask you both this: How do you feel when you're not getting along with each other?"*

> *"I feel bad," Samantha says. "I don't like fighting all the time. I don't know why Max doesn't like me and hits me all the time. I would like to get along better."*

> *"How do you feel about it Max?"*

"I think Samantha is a 'goody goody'. I'm always getting blamed for everything. Why doesn't anyone ever take my side? I think you like her better than you do me."

Dad says: "I'm glad you brought that up. It helps us to know what you're thinking. That must feel awful, to think that we love Samantha more than you. I can see how you might get that idea, because we probably do yell at you more. And I think we're probably wrong to do that. We should change the way we have been handling things. And I feel really sad that you got the impression we favoured Sam over you. But I want you to know that both your mother and I love you. You're very special to us because of who you are." Dad playfully messes Max's hair.

Mom joins in: "Your dad's right. We love you both. Maybe you can both help us figure out a better way to handle these family problems. For instance, when you guys have a disagreement, what do you think we should do about it?"

Neither child responds.

"What would you think if, when you two start to fight, you both leave the room and find a solution to your fight? That way, you won't disturb us with your arguing. You can come back when you've done that. This way we don't have to take sides. And besides, we think you two can figure it out yourselves."

(Mom and Dad will have to spend time at future meetings to teach their children problem resolution (See Problem Solving, Chapter 10). The purpose of this meeting was simply to air their feelings of competition and favouritism.)

"Of course, if you can't find a solution yourselves," says Dad, "we can talk about it at the next family meeting. But I think the main rule we should agree to is that no one in this family hits each other or tattles."

"I like that rule," says Samantha.

"And I like the part about not tattling," says Max. "It sounds fair to me."

Dad say's, "At our next meeting, we can talk about how this is working out."

"I'm so glad we were able to talk about our feelings as a family," says Mom. "You were all very helpful in coming up with the solutions to the problem. If we can do this every week, I'm sure we'll all get along better."

The progress that was made at this meeting involved getting the parents to extricate themselves from showing partiality to one child over another. They also got the children to air their views, as well as commit to a rule about not hitting each other.

Allowing children to resolve their own disagreements

When siblings disagree they are actually learning how to get along with each other. By extension, they are also learning what bothers other people and what it takes to have their friends enjoy playing with them. They have to learn to share, take turns, play by the rules, and not to always have their own way. Although parents often believe that when they intervene they are helping solve the dispute, in actuality they are preventing their children from learning valuable lessons. When parents take sides and allow one child to win over the other, we rob them of the opportunity of learning how to get along. In extreme cases, if the parent plays favourites, one child may feel cheated, and develop a dislike for the sibling, because the sibling managed to get him into trouble and make him look bad. Parents have to develop the skill of learning how to stay out of children's disputes at the time of the fight (unless there is the threat of serious psychological or physical injury), and have faith that their children will be able to resolve their own problems. Later you can talk to them about problem solving techniques they can use to get along better.

You should also be aware of underlying goals that can be the real reason for the fighting. Don't get trapped in giving undue attention or being set up in a power struggle.

Sibling rivalry do's and don't's

- Don't be overly concerned with being fair to all the siblings. Accept the fact that you can never be totally fair all the time. Trying can heighten competition, because the children are learning from you that this IS important.
- Never make comparisons: "Your sister could swim by the age of six."
- Spend a lot of one-on-one time doing something special with each of your children.
- Show a lot of affection to each of your children.
- Ignore instances of insignificant bickering.
- If one child does get hurt during a fight, don't overdo your reaction.
- Remove toys or objects that are being used as weapons during fights.
- Never take sides.

- Don't give your children labels: "You're the athletic one. You're the pretty one."
- Go easy on praise.
- Don't punish your "problem" child.
- Talk about feelings with your children. In particular, let them express their negative feelings.
- Put them all in the same boat. If there is a problem, make them all responsible for finding a solution.
- Encourage your children to help each other.
- Accentuate what is going well between the siblings.
- Teach your children problem solving techniques.
- Encourage tattlers to solve the problem themselves.
- Teach your children the fundamentals of living together: sharing, taking turns, helpfulness, etc.
- Be consistent about ground rules for your family: no hitting, no put downs, etc. Make sure you follow them as well.
- Catch them in the act of being nice to each other.

- When siblings fight, very often one will play the role of the "good" child and one the "bad". This is because each sibling wants to be the favourite of the parents. For this reason, getting involved when siblings fight only increases the rivalry.

- The best antidote to sibling rivalry is to not get involved unless it becomes physically dangerous.

- If you believe a child is feeling that you favour one sibling more than him, spend time with him and talk about his feelings.

- You can minimize sibling rivalry by never showing favouritism.

- Fighting between siblings is not all bad. It is part of the process of learning how to get along with people. This is one more reason to stay out of their disputes.

Problem solving and conflict resolution

Feeling rushed in the morning because they both have to be at work early, Mom and Dad have decided that Jessica (10), and David (8), should make their own lunch, starting immediately. They sat down with them after dinner and told them of this new rule.

"Your Dad and I have decided that it would be a great idea if you two made your own lunches. The kids next door do it and they're the same age as you. You can start tomorrow."

Jessica, who is generally happy to take on new responsibilities, was excited about this, and was already planning her next day's menu. David seemed less *enthused, but not wanting to be shown up by his sister, he grudgingly agreed.*

The parents decided beforehand that, if the children didn't make their own lunch, the consequence would be that they would go hungry. They tell them this and get a murmured agreement. Mom and Dad are thrilled at how easy this was. The next morning, David starts to complain.

"I don't want to make lunch. You make it for me. Why should I have to do it? It's your job!"

Mom is surprised that he is reneging on a promise she thought he made. This quickly turns to anger when he persists. She is very upset at the thought of him going without lunch, but feels it is her duty to let him suffer the consequences. Both David and his mother are furious by the time he leaves (without lunch) for school. The second day, David again refuses to make his lunch. This stalemate goes on for three days. By this time, Mom's anger level tips her off that this has now become a power struggle.

Mom and Dad were trying to do the right thing: teach their children responsibility and use logical consequences, but they made three mistakes:

1. They set the rule arbitrarily without any discussion and with only tenuous agreement from the children (sitting them down and telling them doesn't count).

2. They didn't prepare David for this extra responsibility. They knew of other children his age who were making their own lunch, but ignored his own level of readiness. They also ignored his body language at the meeting, which should have told them he was having

problems with the idea. Up until now, he had never been involved in any kind of cooking or food preparation.

3. Mom was not ready to give up responsibility for David's lunch. She was still emotionally involved in whether he ate lunch or not, which is why the logical consequence of being hungry didn't work. She was, in fact, trying to force him to make his lunch.

Preparing the children for this new responsibility might have worked out better if it had been approached this way:

At the weekly family meeting, Mom could have pointed out that both she and Dad feel very rushed in the morning.

"You know, kids, your dad and I are very busy in the morning trying to get you off to school and ourselves off to work. You already do such a great job of dressing yourselves and setting the breakfast table. Do you think you could help out even more by making your own lunches?" That would really save us a lot of time. What do you think?"

"I guess I could do that," Jessica says. "All my friends make their lunch. In fact, I already know what I'm going to make."

David is less enthusiastic. "OK. I guess maybe I could try it."

Mom says to him: "I appreciate you wanting to help, but you seem a little hesitant. Will this be a problem for you?"

"Well, I'm rushed in the mornings too. I don't think I'm fast enough to make my own lunch right now. It might take me an hour just to wrap my sandwich."

"Well David, what would you think of us making your lunch together until you get the hang of it?"

David looks relieved and agrees. After two weeks of learning the in's and out's of lunch, both David and his mom are ready for him to start doing it himself. Eventually he and his sister make their own and — their parent's — lunches the night before.

David isn't always ready to do the same things as his older sister, who is often better at it than he is. When his mom listened to his concerns and then offered to help, (instead of presenting him with a pre-made decision), it made all the difference in the world.

Problem solving

When children are inexperienced, overwhelmed, or need an answer immediately to a problem, parents can help them to consider available options.

Some suggestions for helping a child would be:

1. Active listening -— first use active listening to understand the difficult situation the child is in.

2. Brainstorming -— encourage the child to come up with as many ideas as he can for the problem. Start by asking questions like this: "Do you have any ideas that might work?" "What could you do to let your friend know how you felt about the name he called you? How

could you make sure he doesn't do it again?" Try to get her to come up with as many ideas as she can.

3. Helping — you can help the child come up with the best idea out of the many possibilities he gave. "From the different ideas you gave, which do you think might be the one you want to use? Let's go through each of your ideas and see which one might work best. OK?"

4. Discussing Probable Results — "If you did that, what might result?"

5. Decision making — now help the child make a decision. "What are you going to do?"

6. Evaluation — "When can we get together and see how it went?"

Whose problem is it?

If you are having a problem with your child, you will have to express to her *your* feelings. Begin by recognizing ownership of the problem. The child is making snacks and leaving a mess in the kitchen. This lack of consideration makes you angry. Recognize that you are having a problem with the outcome of her behaviour. Express to her that "I am angry when I see a messy kitchen."

Acting instead of talking

Our first reaction when there is a problem is to talk about it. But talking is often not effective at the moment a problem is happening. When a parent is attempting to make her child do something and the child refuses to listen, it falls on deaf ears. The child may be not listening in order to get attention or because she wants to engage in an argument, or because she feels she is being controlled or dominated. Therefore, parents need to practise the skills necessary to convince the child that they mean what they say. This is not to say that talking has no place in child rearing, it does, but only after the conflict is over.

Knowing when to leave the room

Conflict is always created by two people and there are always two sides. When one person withdraws from the conflict, the conflict cannot continue. The friction can be considered a battlefield and when the parents leave the battlefield, the child doesn't have anyone to fight with. By taking the "sail out of a child's wind", the child is not in a position to overpower the parent. An excellent place to withdraw is the bathroom because it symbolizes the right to privacy and has a lock on the door. This method is not considered a withdrawal from the child, but a withdrawal from the conflict situation. By not engaging in a pitched battle, parents can continue to maintain their love, affection and friendliness.

Sometimes when withdrawing from the conflict a child's behaviour becomes worse. The reason for this is that in the past the child has successfully engaged the parents in a battle by increasing the intensity. When this occurs, the parent must realize that his strategy is working; the child has lost power over the parent and is making a last stand. This works just as well in public. If a child is demanding that you buy her a toy, for instance, you can withdraw mentally by simply refusing to engage in the argument.

Unreasonable requests

When we have respect for other people, we generally do not make unreasonable demands. With children, because they are younger and because there is usually a lack of respect, our demands sometimes are unreasonable. A good example of this is asking a child to do something, but demanding he do it "right now!" If unreasonable demands are made, a child might feel imposed upon, bossed around, and become rebellious. Conflicts arising out of unreasonable requests can be avoided. Think it through before telling a child what to do.

The way to promote friendliness and have a satisfactory relationship with children is to make your requests few and far between (this does not include the regular jobs and routines the child has agreed to do). Give the child a chance to answer yes or no to the request. An excellent way of determining if requests are reasonable is to put ourselves into the child's shoes and try to determine how we would feel if that request were made of us.

Dad is in the backyard doing his favourite thing — working in the garden. His son, Matthew, has a friend over and they are on the back porch deeply engrossed in a Mechanno set.

"Matthew," Dad calls out. "Would you please go get me my pruning shears from the garage?"

"Matthew frowns. "Ah gee Dad. I'm busy."

"Come on Mat. Go get me my shears. I need them now."

Matthew reluctantly agrees and gets the sheers. A few minutes later, the phone rings, and Dad asks Matthew to answer it. He does but he is getting increasingly frustrated. Ten minutes later Dad has another request.

"Hey Mat. Come here and give me a hand with this rose bush, would you please?"

"For crying out loud Dad! I can't concentrate on what I'm doing. Can't you do it yourself?"

"No. I can't do it myself. And I'm surprised you can't spare the time to help me. Never mind. I'll get somebody else to help me."

Dad wasn't being considerate of Matthew's situation. He could have done the first two things himself. He might have, if he had realized that Matthew was as deeply engrossed in his Mechanno set as he was in his gardening. Then, when he really did need some help (with the rose bush), he would have been justified asking for it. A lot of conflicts arise from lack of consideration of the other person.

Basic principles of resolving conflicts

1. Conflict resolution has to be based upon mutual respect. When a parent fights with a child or imposes his demands, it violates the rights of the child. If the parent allows the child to get her way, it shows a lack of respect for the parent.

2. The healthier the relationship the easier the problem solving.

3. Any interaction between the parent and the child is an agreement between them, even if not on a conscious level. It is important to understand that when we fight, we have both agreed to it. In order to stop fighting, only one person has to decide to stop. Remember, we only have power over our own actions. And, once you have

made the decision to stop fighting, you have created an opportunity to resolve problems differently.

4. Both the parent and child have to accept mutual responsibility for decision making. Each person involved in the problem has the right and the responsibility to contribute solutions. No one can make demands or force her ideas on someone else.

Conflict Resolution

The Six-Step Problem Solving Method (Proposed by John Dewey)

Step One — Defining The Problem

State your problem - "I can't hear Grandma on the phone." "I'm not feeling well." "I'm upset when you fight." This does not make a demand or emphasize your wants, it simply states the problem clearly.

Step Two — Cooperating In Finding Possible Solutions

Each person offers various solutions to the problems and no evaluation of these solutions is discussed. (That comes in Step 3.) All possible solutions are written down. You can even encourage outrageous solutions ("We can all eat dinner on our beds."), because not only is it fun, it helps people to be creative.

Step Three — Evaluating The
Creative Solutions

This is the part that determines which solutions people like and which they want to exclude. Cross off the list any solution that people feel will not work. Everyone can explain why she doesn't like a particular solution, but there is no argument about it. People explain what solutions they feel will be effective in resolving the problem from the solutions that are left. Again, there is no disagreement from others.

Step Four — Consensus Decision Making

Solutions are adopted when everyone agrees that this, or a combination of solutions, would resolve this problem. No solution is accepted unless everyone agrees. If someone doesn't agree with a solution, don't apply pressure but try to get her to give it a try since the others like the idea. Do not use pressure on anyone to give in to an idea. It is important that this is done of her own free will.

Step Five — Agreeing How To Carry
Out The Decision

Discuss what will be done. Who will do it? When should it be done? Where will it take place? How will it get done?

Step Six — Evaluating The Success
Of The Solutions

Agree upon a time to discuss the results. Questions used to evaluate:

- Is the problem over?
- Are you satisfied with the results?
- Was it effective?

If the solution didn't work, then go through the conflict resolution procedure again.

When solutions don't work, it is important to emphasize that this is not an indication of failure. People learn a great deal even when things don't work. Remember to look at the positive side:

- It was a democratic process that included everyone's ideas;
- The group worked together cooperatively;
- They are all becoming better at problem solving through practise;
- The people involved formed a closer relationship;
- They developed the courage to be imperfect. They learned it is all right to make mistakes;
- The children believe they can contribute to the solution of family problems.

Building cooperation

Parents often complain that children are not cooperative. But frequently, by "cooperation" we really mean that children should do what they are told. This is called "cooperation on demand". "If you don't cooperate with me, you are not being cooperative." In the old autocratic culture, demanding cooperation from children was acceptable.

In a democratic culture we cannot demand cooperation, we have to win it. We have to motivate children to want to be helpful because it is best for everyone, not just because we want it. Therefore, cooperation means that each member of the family works towards accomplishing the tasks that are best for all. When we impose our will on children it usually leads to rebellion, not cooperation.

Cooperation is moving together in harmony towards a necessary goal. Every member of the family needs to think in terms of what is best for the family. The question to constantly ask yourself is: What does the situation demand?

Third party interference

Generally speaking, a problem between two people is just that: between those two people and something which *they* have to resolve. By taking sides or interfering, we don't allow the kind of resolution of the problem that can create a stronger relationship. You also risk bringing resentment upon yourself for interfering. Of course it's quite natural to want to come to the rescue of your child when she is experiencing difficulties. There are times when it is appropriate, but you also have to let your children know that you have faith in their ability to solve problems.

The most obvious example of interference is between the parents themselves. It's quite natural that each parent will have her own ideas about parenting. The children recognize this and form a unique relationship with each of the parents. That's why it's not a good idea to fight over child rearing. If the parents fight openly about techniques, the child may be tempted to use the disagreement to form an alliance with one parent against the other. If parents don't attempt to control the other's relationship with the child, the family dynamics will be more wholesome, i.e.; less alliances and manipulation.

Also, unless there is physical or emotional abuse, or the difficulty of the problem is beyond your child's abilities, it is recommended that parents not interfere in their children's relationships with others. In truth, you don't have to worry about children being confused by the different treatments he or she might receive from his or her mother or father, or for that matter, any other relative. Children easily learn to differentiate the expectations of different people.

> *Seven year old Sabrina comes crying to her mother. "Mom, Dad says I can't go to the movies with Caitlan. All I did was say 'so what' but he says I'm talking back too much or something, and that I can't go. He's mean. You told me I could go."*
>
> *Mom puts her arms around her and says: "But you've been planning this movie for a week. It's not fair for him to change your plans like that. I'll talk to him. Now you stop crying. I'll fix this up, don't worry."*
>
> *Sabrina listens as Mom and Dad have a big argument. Although Dad feels he has every right to keep Sabrina from the movies, he backs down to keep peace with his wife. However, he resents his wife's interference and feels he is sometimes ganged up on.*

Sabrina has figured out how to pit one parent against the other in order to get what she wants. Mom should respect the fact that Dad and Sabrina have a relationship, and their differences should remain between the two of them. She should have told her daughter "I'm sorry you're upset with Dad, but you will have to sort it out with him."

Both of these parents have different views of parenting. It would be great if they both agreed, but the reality is that there are always differences of opinion. Mom, for instance, feels that talking about a problem is the best solution, where Dad prefers a punishment approach. Contrary to popular belief, children are not confused by different approaches in parenting styles. They clearly understand each of their parent's views. The interpersonal dynamics of the above scene are interesting: Sabrina gets her father angry at her, who then uses a form of punishment. Sabrina then tattles to her mother about how mean Dad was, and Mom asserts herself as the ultimate authority, overruling her husband's decision and allying herself with the child against him.

The same goes for problems with a neighbour, a relative or a teacher. The parents should be there to listen, support and help problem solve, but essentially it is the child's relationship and she is responsible for it. Once again, you need to send the message that you trust your child to handle life's problems.

> *Thirteen year old Eric joins the local hockey team. He goes to the first few practises and games but loses interest and begins skipping more and more. The team rule is that if you miss more than three practises, you are off the team. Eric knows this but he misses three practises anyway. When his team makes it to the finals, Eric's interest is rekindled. He pleads with the coach to let him rejoin the team but the coach is adamant: "Those are the rules, Eric. If I let you back it wouldn't be fair to the other players who did attend the practises."*
>
> *Eric asks his parents to intercede, pointing out that he is a skilful player, and that he missed the practises only because he had extra school assignments to do. His parents accept his excuses and go to see the coach. He tries to remain firm, but Eric's parents persist, even threatening to go to the team's sponsors (who do business with Eric's mother), to get them to pull their sponsorship. The coach relents and Eric rejoins the team.*

Even though Eric got what he wanted, his parents did him a great disservice. Instead of letting him learn the hard lessons of life about fulfilling commitments and experiencing the consequences of his actions, they have taught him to take the easy way out. Mom and Dad need to stop trying to arrange the world to please Eric. Outside of the moral question here, they should realize that they will not always be there to smooth the way for him. He is about to go out into the world, thinking that he can do what he wants: that the rules don't apply to him.

To help children solve problems, use the following techniques:
1. Active Listening
2. Brainstorming — Get your children to come up with as many possible solutions as they can.
3. Helping — Help them pick the best solution out of the ones they brainstormed.
4. Discuss possible results — "If you did that, what might happen?"
5. Decision making — "What are you going to do?"
6. Evaluation — "Let's get together and see how it went."

• Take ownership of the problem. Learn to express your feelings to your child. If he is being disrespectful, tell him: "I don't want to stay in the room with you when you act like this."

• Act instead of talk. Talking is not effective at the moment the problem is occurring. Talk about what happened after the dust has settled.

• It takes two to have a fight. If your child is determined to fight with you, withdraw from the conflict — leave the room or lock yourself in the bathroom. This should not be seen as withdrawal from the child, but the conflict itself. If you notice that the child's behaviour is becoming worse, you know the strategy is working.

• Rely on routine and consistency more than constant requests. Try not to demand that things be done RIGHT NOW! Put yourself in your child's shoes and see how you would react to such a demand.

- The Basic Principles of Conflict Resolution
  1. Conflict resolution is based on mutual respect.
  2. The healthier the relationship, the easier the problem solving.
  3. If parent and child fight, it is because they have agreed to fight.

- The Six Steps to Conflict Resolution
  1. Define the problem
  2. Cooperate in finding a solution
  3. Evaluate solutions
  4. Make decisions by consensus
  5. Agree to carry out decisions
  6. Evaluate the success of the decisions

- In a democratic culture, a problem involving two people is *their* problem and they should be allowed to find a solution themselves. This is especially important in problems between one parent and a child.

Competence and independence

Y ou feel competent when you know you have the skills to handle the challenges that life throws your way. Every time you learn a new skill, you feel better about yourself and more in control of your life. Think of the vast number of skills that adults pick up during their lives. Even relatively mundane skills, such as being able to fix a leaking faucet or do your own tax returns, bring a measure of competence and, therefore, independence. That's because it feels good to know you can handle things. This goes double for children.

Young children learn more in the first few years of their life than any of us will ever cram into that short space of time again. A child's mind is like a sponge that literally soaks up knowledge and skills. Your job as a parent is to facilitate this incredible explosion of learning. We know that children have a tremendous capacity to learn, and we also know that self esteem is linked to feelings of competence. We can best help them learn, as well as bolster their self esteem, by teaching them skills. Children are born with innate courage, and the natural inclination of young children is to watch and imitate what other people are doing. When a child pours his own milk he feels capable. Remember how proud you felt when you learned to ride a two-wheeler? Sometimes all a parent has to do is *allow* the child to learn a new skill.

> *Every morning, two and half year old Daniel watches his mother and father pour cereal and milk for themselves and the other children. One morning, Daniel starts whining when his mother begins to pour his cereal.*
>
> *"I do it mommy. I do it."*
>
> *He takes the cereal box and pours, spilling some on the table but essentially doing it himself. He feels very proud. This was a skill that he learned simply by watching how it was done. He will obviously need to practise this in order to perfect it, but he didn't need a specific lesson.*

Although children learn a great deal through observation, some skills have to be taught and practised, i.e.; making beds, using the washing machine, babysitting and taking care of the dog. Parents need to be alert for signs that the child is ready to learn a skill, like Daniel pouring the cereal in the above scenario. When a child says "I want to try this", you should let him try (unless it is something that is too dangerous).

In addition to learning through observation there are other, more indirect ways of teaching your child. Opening the door and saying something like "It looks like rain. I better bring my umbrella today," is an excellent way of teaching your child to use an umbrella without relying on commands. Your own mistakes can also be a great chance for indirect teaching: "Oh oh. I left my toast in the toaster too long and it burned."

When specific lessons are in order, set aside a specific time for teaching them, when neither you nor the children are pressured. Remember, children have vivid imaginations and love role playing and acting, so use these when teaching them. For instance, "Let's pretend that all of your toys are soldiers and are marching into the toy box," is a good way to teach them how to put things away.

Always make sure that not too much is done for younger children, especially by the older siblings. It's easy for the youngest in the family to be the least competent, simply because he is surrounded by so many competent people.

Randy wants to tie his shoes like everyone else in the family, but he is only five years old and can't quite get the hang of it. Mom is in a hurry to get to play group and starts to put on Randy's shoes.

"Wait Mom," he says. "I want to tie them up."

Mom gives a deep sigh and says, "OK. Here's what you do. Take this lace and wrap it around this one like this."

"Like this?" asks Randy.

"No, no. Like THIS."

Randy tries again but gets it wrong. Mom looks at her watch and is about to show him again when she stops. "You know what Randy? We don't have enough time right now. But I'll tell you what. As soon as we get everyone off to school tomorrow, I'll teach you exactly how to tie your own shoelaces.

That night Mom takes an old picture frame and tacks a piece of material down each side. She makes button holes in both pieces and strings laces through them. The next morning, she presents this new "toy" to Randy and spends a half an hour teaching him how to tie a bow.

Mom was much more successful with her second approach than her first. She not only planned a good time for the lesson to take place, but also did the necessary prep work as well. Not only did Randy learn to tie his shoes, but Mom signalled her faith in his ability to learn by taking the necessary time to teach him properly.

Observe your children carefully and see how they learn best. If they resist being given lessons, rely more on indirect methods.

Overprotection

Parents love their children and have difficulty watching them experience unpleasant situations. However, we cannot protect our children from all of life's hardships, nor would it be good for them if we did. Our aim should be to equip children with courage by emphasizing their strengths. Ironically, the more we over protect children, the greater the possibility harm could come to them. The child who is never allowed to cross streets by himself can never learn to be alert to traffic. We have to make sure we don't keep our children helpless, weak and dependent on us. *Over*protection is just that, one step beyond the level of protection children need.

The response of children to overprotection depends on the individual child. Some children allow this kind of pampering, and become helpless in dealing with problems. Other children, who want to be independent, fight back.

By overprotecting children we arrange life to be perfect for them. We coddle and cushion them until they come to see life as one long, easy stretch of road. But we can't protect them from everything, especially as they become older. They can then become angry at the world when situations arise that they are not comfortable with. On the other hand, giving your child responsibilities he can't handle can be equally frustrating. Knowing how much to let your child experience on her own is a balancing act. Think of yourself as a filter that allows your children to experience more difficult situations as they grow and can handle them.

The dangers of pity

Children have to learn to take disappointments in life and they are better able to do this if we avoid pitying them. We cannot protect a child from suffering, for suffering is a part of life. The best thing we can do is to help a child learn to tolerate and manage difficult circumstances.

Feeling sorry for a child is very damaging even if it appears to be justified. Children are very sensitive to their parents' attitudes even though the parents may not verbally express them. Therefore, if we feel pity for a child, the child may take this to heart and feel sorry for herself. If a child falls down and scrapes her knee, a great show of sympathy by the adults will usually result in a greater show of suffering by the child. The idea is to replace pity with reassurance. The more self pity we feel, the less courageous we are. When others feel sorry for us, we may feel overwhelmed and powerless. Children may even become convinced that life owes them something. At any rate, whenever anyone feels sorry for himself there is a deep unhappiness.

Remember, there is a difference between empathy and pity. Empathy demonstrates an understanding of how the child feels and how difficult it is for them. Pity implies they are weak. It sends the message that you feel sorry for him: "You poor thing, I know how much you suffer and I'll try to make up for what has happened." This is particularly easy to fall into when the child is hurt by the divorce or separation of his parents. Admittedly a difficult problem for the child, pity can compound it ten fold by making the child feel hard done by and resentful. Pity can make it much harder for the child to come to terms with the divorce

During the annual winter parent-teacher meeting, Anna's grade one teacher and Anna's mother are discussing her progress. Anna's parents have recently separated, something she is having a hard time dealing with.

"Since the separation, I've noticed that Anna has been less interested in her school work and much more aggressive with her friends," says Anna's teacher.

"Well, obviously Anna is feeling very sad about her dad not being there," explains her mother. "And who could blame her, poor thing? When I was young, nobody's father just up and left the family. She's going through an extremely hard time right now, and we have to make allowances."

"I agree, this must be a difficult time," says the teacher. "Maybe we can work together to help Anna to get through this."

"But how can she get through it? She'll always be from a broken home now. It's going to be her cross to bear."

"I can make an appointment with the school counsellor for her," offers the teacher.

"No, no. Anna is too distraught right now. I think the best thing would be to leave her alone and make allowances."

When Anna's teacher tried to take constructive steps to help her deal with the problems in her life, her mother countered with pity. Anna does need understanding and support. Ironically though, her mother's attitude that Anna can't handle the cards life has dealt her is keeping her from getting the support she needs. Both guilt and pity are emotions that have no place in child rearing. Anna's mother should also allow her to maintain a relationship with her father, and focus on creating a happy home life together with her. It could take up to a year to adjust to these new circumstances, and she may want to use community support groups at this critical juncture.

Coping with children's fear

We all experience fear. Fear can be helpful. For instance, it makes us cautious when in dangerous situations. But fear can also be debilitating. In general, it is wise not to cater to unfounded fears. In most everyday situations, a few words of comfort is all it should take to calm a frightened child. The danger is that children can quickly learn that their fears have a powerful control over their parents. And it is easy for parents to overreact, because when children express fears, they appear so small and vulnerable. The vicious circle is that through fears, children can control their parents by getting them to over protect them. Yet the more we protect, the more the child is convinced of his lack of competence to handle the situation.

Fear can also be utilized by a child to gain attention and put the parents in her service. For example, children who are afraid of the dark can keep their parents by their bedside until they fall asleep.

> Four year old Alfie suddenly developed a fear of ants one summer. "Mommy! Daddy! Bugs! Help! Help!"
>
> No matter what they were doing, his parents had to come running every time an ant got into the house or entered Alfie's sandbox.

Alfie's fear is a real one, but catering to it will not make it go away, and may even intensify it. Alfie's parents need to firmly reassure him that the ants won't harm him. They then need to stop responding to his unfounded calls for help. To help him overcome his worries, they can ask him if he would like to get a book on ants from the library in order to find out more about them, or even take a trip to the local science centre. At any rate, he should not be able to use his fear of ants to keeps his parents monopolized.

The best way to help children overcome fear is to build up their self confidence and to help them accept discomfort and face events themselves. Don't overprotect and don't become manipulated by their fears. By not being impressed with their fears, we avoid instilling in them feelings of timidity and anxiety. Show children you have confidence in them; that they are strong enough, and have sufficient understanding to work through fears.

Routine and consistency

Think of a child as a train and the tracks as daily routine. The train can't move at all without the tracks just as a child can't negotiate the daily needs and challenges of the day without routines.

Most of us need routines in order to feel comfortable. We like to know what to expect. This is why routines are such a big part of our lives. Children especially need them. When children aren't sure what's going to happen next, they become insecure and demanding. Routines create predictability, as well as a feeling of security and order. There are times of the day (bedtime and mornings), when routines encourage the smooth flow of activity. Children feel more in control when they know what they are supposed to do and what is going to happen. For example, when children know what time they are going to eat, they don't have to continually ask the parents, "When are we going to eat?" They already know when. Not knowing what is coming creates feelings of anxiety. There is so much in life that children don't understand, or that seem controlled by the whim of adults. But routines are a way of making most everyday aspects of life make sense to children. Therefore, it is the obligation of parents to set up routines so that all members of the family can function comfortably.

> *Every night the McCarty family prepares for bed. At eight o'clock the TV is turned off and the bath is run. The two boys — five year old Darcy and seven year John, run up stairs and get into the bath. Sometimes, they plead to stay up late or try to skip the bath, but their parents have always held firm to the routine unless there was a very good reason to change it.*
>
> *After the bath, the boys automatically get into their pajamas and select a bed time story. They've done this so many times they don't even think about it. Lights out is always 15 minutes later.*

The McCarty's have never had a serious bedtime problem. That's because the order of the bedtime routine has become second nature to their children. It almost wouldn't occur to them to do anything else. They enjoy knowing what to expect, so they don't seriously test the limits. Many difficult situations parents encounter with their children (bedtimes, mornings, meal times, etc.), can be solved by creating predictable patterns. However, when routine is established it should be made for the convenience of all family members, not just the parents.

Consistency, like routine, provides the boundaries and limitations a child needs for security. When we are consistent, we follow through with the rules. When we say something is going to happen ("If you guys aren't finished your bath by 8:30, there won't be enough time for a story."), we have to let the child know we mean it. That's why it's never wise to make threats you know you can't follow through on, such as: "If you're not ready in two minutes, I'm going without you." When we violate rules or allow them to be broken, the child will be confused as to whether order is really important. They don't know which rules are important and which aren't. By testing the rules, they may become quite rebellious as they argue and fight back. What parents must remember is, if a rule is made, it is important and, therefore, must be followed through.

S U M M A R Y

- All of us need to learn skills in order to feel confident and able to deal with life. Young children especially want to and are capable of learning a vast amount. Our job as parents is to facilitate this explosion of learning in our children.

- One way to teach children is to let them observe you. If they see you clearing the table after a meal, they will eventually want to do it too. Your job is to let them do it, even if they make mistakes.

- Another way to teach children is by indirect means. For example, let them see you taking too many bags out of the car, and saying: "This is too heavy. I better make two trips." Allowing your children to see you making mistakes is also a good way for them to learn: "Look at that. I wasn't watching what I was doing and now I've made a mess."

- Be alert for signs your children are ready to learn.

- Use your children's imagination and love of role playing to help them learn new skills.

- Make sure that the youngest of the family — surrounded as he is by people who are more competent then he is — doesn't grow up feeling incompetent.

- Set aside quiet, un-pressured time for teaching skills.

- Don't overprotect your child. Overprotection is done by parents who want to shield their child from the suffering of life. This is understandable, however overprotection will ironically cause more suffering because the child grows up unable to deal with life. Instead, act as a filter to allow your child to experience hardships, while protecting him from the serious dangers and hazards of life he can't handle.

- Know the difference between pity and empathy. Feeling pity for a child makes him feel weak. Empathy lets the child know you understand what he is going through.

- Fear is useful because it keeps us away from dangerous situations, but children can use fear to manipulate their parents. Don't cater to children's fears. Instead, build up their feelings of self confidence.

- Children need and want routines in their life. Routines create a sense of predictability and order. They also make problem times (bedtime, mornings, etc.) run smoother because everyone knows what is expected.

- The glue that keeps routines together is consistency.
  Consistency means being firm about rules and letting your children know you mean it. Otherwise, they won't know what is important and what isn't. This confusion often leads to rebellion and arguing.

IN CLOSING

We hope that reading this book and familiarizing yourself with the concepts and strategies it contains, will help you have an even better relationship with your children. Don't be discouraged if your situation doesn't completely turn around immediately, or if your child's behaviour takes a turn for the worse after a period of improvement. The Practical Parenting Program is based on tried and tested principles that will work for you and your family if practised consistently.

You should also keep in mind that learning how to be a better parent is no reflection on you or how your own parents raised you. The truth is, everyone, no matter what your present situation, can benefit from parenting programs.

To get the most out of this program, keep these important concepts in mind:

✓ *Always strive to understand why your child is being uncooperative.*

✓ *Be consistent when applying the principles you have learned in the Practical Parenting Program.*

✓ *Really listen to your child, and let him know that you are listening to him.*

✓ *Hold regular family meetings. Use the meetings to foster better communication, bring the family closer, and solve problems in a way that satisfies everyone.*

✓ *Above all, be patient with yourself. Being a parent is the hardest job you will ever have. But it is also the most rewarding, especially if you acquire the skills to do it with all of the ability you and your children deserve.*

We at Practical Parenting Program Inc. are committed to upholding the information set forth in this book. Please understand that the actions and presentations of the Practical Parenting Facilitators are separate from the Practical Parenting Program and are not under our control; however, if you should ever have a problem at one of the parenting groups, we hope that you will please inform us so that we may try to rectify the situation for you and for future participants.

Teach Practical Parenting,
A Message From Stanley Shapiro

We hope you have enjoyed this edition of Practical Parenting. Would you like to learn how to teach the Practical Parenting Program and work either part time or full time in the public and private sector. Qualified candidates must be professionals (i.e., teacher, nurse, early childhood educator, pediatrician, or have a Bachelor's degree or equivalent.) Interested candidates must also participate in a screening process.

To become a Practical Parenting Program Leader, call or write the Practical Parenting Program Inc. Toronto, Canada

The goal of the Practical Parenting Program is to create the awareness that parenting is the most important job in the world and have all parents be trained for this most important job.

We are currently translating the Practical Parenting Program into many other languages so that every parent may have access to these essential skills, thereby, bettering the lives of children. Please contact Stanley Shapiro directly, or any of the representatives of the Practical Parenting Program to get involved.

Practical Parenting
Book Order Form

To order extra copies of Practical Parenting, A Common Sense Guide to Raising Cooperative, Self Reliant and Loving Children, *send a self-addressed envelope and enclose only a personal cheque or money order (do not send cash) made payable to:*

Practical Parenting Program Inc.
Harding P.O. Box 32142
Richmond Hill, Ontario, Canada L4C 9S3
GST #886582477RT

Practical Parenting Book Order Form

Tear Off And Include

Name
(Please Print Clearly)

Complete Address

City _____ Prov/State _____ PC/Zip_____

_____ copies of the Practical Parenting Text x $20.00

_____ copies of the Practical Parenting Study Guide
(8 Session Guide) x $19.00

_____ copies of the Practical Parenting Advanced Study Guide
(6 Session Guide) x $19.00

Prices include Ontario Sales Tax, shipping and handling

My total payment enclosed $_____ by ☐ cheque or ☐ money order

Please allow approximately four to six weeks for delivery